UNCOVERING
THE SECRETS OF
BIBLE
PROPHECY

JEFF KINLEY

HARVEST HOUSE PUBLISHERS
EUGENE, OREGON

Cover by Bryce Williamson

Cover photos © Tryaging/iStockphoto; Sudowoodo/Getty

Published in association with William K. Jensen Literary Agency, 119 Bampton Court, Eugene, Oregon 97404.

Uncovering the Secrets of Bible Prophecy
Copyright © 2018 Jeff Kinley
Published by Harvest House Publishers
Eugene, Oregon 97408
www.harvesthousepublishers.com

ISBN 978-0-7369-7488-2 (pbk.)
ISBN 978-0-7369-7489-9 (eBook)

Library of Congress Cataloging-in-Publication Data

Names: Kinley, Jeff, author.
Title: Uncovering the secrets of Bible prophecy / Jeff Kinley.
Description: Eugene : Harvest House Publishers, 2018.
Identifiers: LCCN 2018009563 (print) | LCCN 2018020745 (ebook) | ISBN
   9780736974899 (ebook) | ISBN 9780736974882 (pbk.)
Subjects: LCSH: Bible—Prophecies.
Classification: LCC BS647.3 (ebook) | LCC BS647.3 .K56 2018 (print) | DDC
   220.1/5—dc23
LC record available at https://lccn.loc.gov/2018009563

Printed in the United States of America

18 19 20 21 22 23 24 25 26 / BP-GL / 10 9 8 7 6 5 4 3 2 1

For Henry

Contents

Introduction
Why Study Bible Prophecy? 7

Chapter 1
Understanding the Nature of Prophecy:
Its Essence and Divine Purpose 11

Chapter 2
Don't Misread the Signs: The Six Big Mistakes
People Make with Prophecy. 23

Chapter 3
Developing Biblical Discernment:
Meet the New "Sons of Issachar" 37

Chapter 4
Spotting Counterfeit Truth: Fake News and
False Prophets, Then and Now. 55

Chapter 5
Cracking the Bible Code: Proven Principles
of Prophetic Interpretation 75

Chapter 6
Exploring Scripture's Unfulfilled Prophecies:
Christian Hype or Coming Reality? 91

Chapter 7
Examining the Major Views on Prophecy:
Contradictions, Clarity, and Consensus. 109

Chapter 8
Investigating "Prophecy Apologetics": End-Times
Evidence for Skeptical Minds. 131

Chapter 9
Building Up the Body of Christ: The Barnabas
Principle of Prophecy 153

Chapter 10
Preparing for Jesus's Return: Possessing a Certain
Hope and a Pure Heart 169

Endnotes 183

Introduction:

Why Study Bible Prophecy?

Bible prophecy.

The Enigma code of Christianity. And to many, a seemingly unsolvable Revelation-style Rubik's Cube. Like a puzzle with more than a few pieces missing, this subject continues to arouse interest and garner international attention.

Including yours.

Actually, Bible prophecy should interest you because it, above most everything else on planet Earth, is very interesting. One reason for this is that we currently find ourselves living in perilous and uncertain days. A strange moment in time, for sure. But regardless of whether you're simply at the curious stage or are a seasoned student of eschatology—either way, you still want to know more. And that's a good thing. It's also the mark of a true disciple of Jesus (Matthew 11:29; 2 Peter 3:18).[1]

These days, more and more people find themselves drawn toward the apocalyptic—including those who frequent conferences, read books, magazines, and blogs, and watch movies with this theme. Even novels on the subject have become national bestsellers. But the common thread knitting all these people together is that, like you, they long to know what God's Word says about future things. They want to know what's coming and, if possible, discover a general idea of *when*.

More importantly, many seek the practical difference those prophecies can make in their lives...right now.

But this desire to engage prophecy is not some accidental curiosity. No, I believe it has been placed in you by divine design. Therefore, your pursuit of answers is actually more by providence than by your own plan. Naturally, if there *is* such a prophetic future as described in Scripture (and I believe there is), you should seek to find out what it will be like. You want to know how to navigate through the prophetic fog that blankets our time. But while eager to know what's on God's future calendar, you also desire to guard yourself from being duped by sensationalism and those who propagate the prophetic version of "fake news."

If that's where this book finds you, then you're in a good place. You're a part of a unique tribe, a band of believers not content to drift aimlessly in the shallow, lazy river of ignorance and mediocrity. You simply don't have time for that. You *must* dig deeper, discover more, and live purposefully.

Prophecy culture is growing, partially because it's becoming obvious, even to secular minds, that we are likely living in earth's end times.[2] The world stage continues preparing itself for the end of days as we ramp up toward Revelation's realities. And among Christians, you can expect this heightened prophetic interest to only become greater in the days to come.

But amid all the hoopla and *aha* experiences associated with engaging Scripture's truths about the last days, a key component is often left behind. What's omitted or overlooked while wading through Revelation's judgments and musings about "666" is how Christians can be certain all these things will actually come to pass. What do we really know? And what is still unclear, even to prophecy experts? How is someone like you supposed to approach the Bible and interpret these incredible predictions? What skills does it require? What pitfalls should you avoid? And what traps must you watch out for?

That's part of what this book will help you identify.

From God's perspective, prophecy goes way beyond merely predicting things. Scripture's prophetic word also reveals important truths about God's character, His values, and His relationship with humankind. And it provides practical benefits critical for you and your life *right now*. For embedded within Bible prophecy is a spiritual treasure waiting to be discovered and enjoyed, a storehouse of future truth meant to transform you in the present tense.

My prayer is that *Uncovering the Secrets of Bible Prophecy* will help you experience both the joy of discovery as well as the benefit of personal enrichment. You'll discover that Bible prophecy's "secrets" are not actually hidden after all, but laid out in plain sight whenever you open your Bible. Aside from satisfying your prophetic taste buds, these truths will also empower your life as you follow Christ in these troubling times. I trust your mind and spirit will be stimulated and refreshed as you read.

Finally, God's prophecies are not only true and certain, they're also good...and good for you. He who holds the future designed His prophetic truth to make you a better worshipper.

And with no time to waste, let's get started with the first key.

Chapter 1

Understanding the Nature of Prophecy

Its Essence and Divine Purpose

He said, "Write, for these words are faithful and true."
REVELATION 21:5

Bible prophecy is a *thing*. A real thing, according to Scripture. And something that radically affects the lives of those who engage with it. Of course, practically speaking, if there are no biblical prophecies to anticipate, then Christians should just keep on doing church and living their lives for God as best as they can. Whatever eventually *does* happen, happens. After all, God's in charge, right? So why even bother thinking about the future? *Que sera, sera.* And no amount of wishful thinking or prophetic speculation about potential coming events will alter His plan. Besides, no one really knows the future…right?

Wrong.

I believe we can know what is going to happen. In fact, we already do. And it's written down in a centuries-old document just waiting for us to discover it. That's because prophecy is both *in there* (the Bible) and *out there* (the future). God has already revealed it to us in His Word. And best of all, He wants us to know about it, respond to it, and let it revolutionize our lives.

Reading the Writings

I come from a large extended family. My dad was one of nine brothers, so there were lots of men I called "uncle." One of those men, my uncle Floyd, never learned to read very well. Growing up during the Great Depression, Floyd decided early on in elementary school that "readin' and writin'" weren't his thing. He never went past the fourth grade, opting instead to stay home and help out around the house, eventually joining the workforce in his teenage years. Though he functioned well enough to get by, Floyd was nevertheless semi-dependent on others to help him read the newspaper or an occasional magazine. On into his later years, the gentle-spirited man would often hand me a newspaper, then with a wink and a smile say, "Hey, Pete," (Floyd called everybody Pete) "read that article to me. I left my glasses at home." Or "I was absent the day they taught readin' at school." Looking back, Floyd may also have suffered from a learning disability. Regardless, ask any of my 40 or so cousins who their favorite uncle was, and to a person they'll point to Uncle Floyd. Just weeks before his passing from cancer, I had the privilege of leading my dear uncle to faith in Jesus. He cried out to God in simple faith, and He answered. Thankfully, you don't have to be well educated to call on the name of the Lord for salvation.

Floyd's lack of education reminds me of many Christians who are functionally illiterate when it comes to the Bible. It's not that they can't read it. It's just that their ability to handle the Word is handicapped by the fact that they have neglected the Scriptures in their daily lives. You may be in a strong Bible-teaching church or have an extensive knowledge of God's Word. If so, you are by far the exception and not the rule.

According to Lifeway Research, only 19 percent of American churchgoers read their Bibles daily. And among teenagers, only 3 percent read them each day, though seven out of ten own a Bible. There are several plausible explanations for such dismal numbers.

Many have simply never been taught how to read and understand the Bible. Some pastors spoon-feed their flocks with feel-good, self-empowering messages, and yet fail to equip their people to become self-feeders (Ephesians 4:11-16). You could add laziness, busyness, apathy, and sin to the list of reasons as well. But regardless of the factors, here we are. Over 80 percent of churchgoing adults are not regularly nourishing themselves with the Word of God. Though they may spend time with other Christians and listen to uplifting music or even Bible-teaching podcasts, these are not replacements for interacting with God one-on-one through His written revelation. Though not characteristic of every church, multiply this mass malnourishment by the roughly 250,000 Protestant churches in America, and you end up with tens of millions of professing believers who are biblically nonfunctional. That means someone else has to cut up their spiritual meat and do the chewing for them. These Christians lack the skills to navigate their way through a book of the Bible or to interact with theological truths found in Scripture. It also makes them much more susceptible to embracing false teaching and idolatrous lies about God. That's because biblical illiteracy logically leads to theological bankruptcy and guaranteed spiritual anemia. And it shows in our culture, where our gospel light has been dimmed and our moral influence diminished.

But as we examine Scripture, we see that this disease of doctrinal deficiency is not a recent phenomenon. It's precisely why Paul exhorted Pastor Timothy to be "constantly nourished on the words of the faith and of the sound doctrine which you have been following" (1 Timothy 4:6). Without an accurate knowledge of Scripture and regular encounters with it, our chances of growth are virtually nil. We effectually die, though we still function. Like spiritual zombies.

Perhaps nowhere is this epidemic more clearly seen than when it comes to Bible prophecy. Many Christians find themselves at a loss when attempting to articulate anything remotely resembling what the Bible says about the end times. And though the vast majority of evangelicals believe we are living in the last days, we really don't seem to care that much. In many churches, our Sunday morning attempts to reach the lost have trumped our mandate to "make disciples...teaching them to observe all that I commanded you" (Matthew 28:18-20). Instead of "equipping the saints for the work of service" (Ephesians 4:12), our consumer-oriented, performance-driven, entertain-me church services have inundated us with what theologian Charles Ryrie once referred to as an "eschatological agnosticism." Translated: Christians simply don't know what the Bible says about the end times. And worse, we don't seem to be bothered by that fact. We don't understand the times because we're too busy trying to *survive* the times!

However, ironically, Revelation and other Scriptures related to the end times were meant to help us do just that. In fact, they go way beyond just helping us get by. This area of biblical truth is one of God's divinely designed means to help us *thrive* in the midst of these dark days in which we live.

The nature of prophecy is that (1) it is divine in origin, meaning it comes not from man's fantastical imagination but from God Himself, and (2) it involves the foretelling of events, both from a national (Israel and Old Testament) and global (Revelation) perspective. And in the end times, the two will overlap.

Rather than being a mere curiosity, Bible prophecy takes up a significant portion of God's Word (28 percent). It's just as legitimate as the Hebrew poetry of Psalms, the narrative Gospel of John, and the didactic Epistle to the Romans. In prophecy, we discover divine promises, predestined predictions, and unconditional provisions given by God concerning the fate of the world, the state of the church, the rebirth and return of the nation Israel, and the future of humankind. In our Lord's prophetic texts, we are given unique insight into His character and the righteous outworking of His eternal plan.

So why would a child of God shy away from such a rich treasure of truth? And how can a lover of Scripture blatantly ignore such a significant portion of the Bible, including hundreds of prophecies yet to be fulfilled? How could we ever view prophecy as merely a spiritual hobby for certain Christians, treating it as one of many menu options in a scriptural buffet? Truthfully, if you remove the prophetic genre from the Bible, you cut out about one-third of all Scripture! If the Bible were a map of the United States, that would be like erasing 16 states. But no worries, you'd still have 34 left, right? This is preposterous!

Eschatology Road

All that being said, I can understand why Bible prophecy seems so hard for most Christians. Eschatology (the study of the end times) can be very *un*like those warm and comforting passages we underline and highlight elsewhere in Scripture. Like two magnets, our hearts and these passages are sometimes irresistibly drawn to one another, forming a strong bond and connection. But turn the page and you may encounter another kind of biblical truth, one producing an almost repelling response. Some prophetic passages can seem prickly and therefore tough to embrace. Honestly, as we fast-forward to history's coming season of judgment and wrath, we encounter some troubling truths in the Word. And because we typically like to keep things positive and upbeat in church, we lean toward those Scriptures that bring us happiness, not heartache. Though this is understandable, it's not biblical.

But can you imagine what would've happened if the Old Testament prophets had taken this approach? What if, in heralding the ancient, prophetic revelation, those tasked with leading God's people had simply left out the heavy, uncomfortable stuff? Perhaps instead of being known as the "Weeping Prophet," Jeremiah could have become the "Positive Prophet" by telling Israel how to have a good self-image or a prosperous life. Nathan didn't really have to face down King David regarding his adulterous affair with Bathsheba and his murder of her husband, did he? That might make him upset. Instead, why not just tell the king, "Okay, look, so you made some unwise choices. We all mess up every now and then. Just try not to do it again, okay?" Rather than confronting and condemning Herod's marriage to his brother's wife, John the Baptist (the last official Old Testament prophet) could have shared with the newlywed couple some helpful tips on having a happy marriage.

Obviously, those are ridiculous examples. "*All* Scripture is inspired by God" and that includes the desirable as well as the difficult truths (2 Timothy 3:16-17). Like the double-edged sword that Scripture is, it comforts and heals as powerfully as it cuts and wounds (Hebrews 4:12). And even though eschatology contains some very unpleasant future happenings, the endgame of prophecy is that our Savior and King is victorious, our sin nature eradicated, our salvation and glorification completed, and our destiny secured. Plus, we reign with Jesus forever! God wins! And we get to share in His joy and celebration. How can these coming realities be anything other than positive and uplifting?

Even so, I do get it. I know why "all that Revelation stuff" seems above most Christians' pay grade. During my 30 years of pastoring, I have observed some of the big reasons why the majority of Christians bypass the sometimes bumpy and uncomfortable road of prophecy. Allow me to articulate each of these reasons for you.

1. "Prophecy is really difficult to interpret and understand."

After all, there are symbols, metaphors, similes, cryptic words, and "hidden" meanings. There are allusions, historical references, seemingly undecipherable word-pictures, and expositional enigmas. All these combined create a sort of Rubik's Cube, and everybody knows only geniuses can solve those things. So, to the average believer, prophecy can seem like a very long game of unsolvable riddles. Rated "E" for expert. Ever felt like that?

2. "I've never heard much teaching on this subject by my pastor."

Tragically, a small percentage of pastors equip their people with solid teaching in this area of theology, and there are many reasons why they avoid the subject altogether (see endnote for the Top Ten

Reasons Why Pastors Don't Preach on Bible Prophecy).[1] One of those reasons is that they themselves were not taught much eschatology in their seminary experience. Other pastors are bi-vocational or have no formal biblical training at the graduate level, and so they may feel inadequate to effectively tackle the subject. And without great training, a pastor must teach himself or be a diligent student of exposition and theology. Most bi-vocational pastors don't have the luxury of time to devote to this amount of study. Since church members form their spiritual values from topics taught by their pastors, they, too, end up either neglecting prophecy or seeking teaching and insight from various outside sources. But part of a pastor-teacher's calling is to "equip the saints" so they can become doctrinally sound and spiritually mature (Ephesians 4:11-16). Like Paul, ministers are to preach the "whole purpose of God" (Acts 20:27). The apostle knew that in the last days, it will become passé to preach the whole truth of God's Word. This is one reason he wrote to his young pastor friend, Timothy,

> I solemnly charge you in the presence of God and of Christ Jesus, who is to judge the living and the dead, and by His appearing and His kingdom: preach the word; be ready in season and out of season; reprove, rebuke, exhort, with great patience and instruction. For the time will come when they will not endure sound doctrine; but wanting to have their ears tickled, they will accumulate for themselves teachers in accordance to their own desires, and will turn away their ears from the truth and will turn aside to myths. But you, be sober in all things, endure hardship, do the work of an evangelist, fulfill your ministry (2 Timothy 4:1-5).

As a pastor for three decades, there were times when I found it awkward and inconvenient to preach certain passages or truths from Scripture. I would've preferred a more positive message, but my calling and duty demanded that I preach the next passage. Inconvenience does not exempt pastors from certain truths, regardless of the difficulty of the truth or people's feelings or responses. What I discovered, though, was that the Holy Spirit always accompanied His Word, illuminating the hearts and minds of seeking Christians and helping them to process His Word, even when it was uncomfortable.

Some leaders in the church today view eschatology as an unnecessary distraction from more central, core doctrines. And understandably, every sermon should not be about the end times. But in an age when Bible prophecy appears to be headed toward fulfillment, it is critical for Christians to hear a clear Word from God concerning the state of the church and the destiny of our world. Sadly, millions of presumably hungry Christians remain confused, mistaken, or stuck in a fog concerning God's prophetic plan and its implications in these last days.

3. "I'm afraid of Revelation and end-times prophecy. It scares me."

I've actually heard this from Christians as to why they steer clear of Revelation. They avoid it like a dark alley or a giant pothole in the road. As such, the last book of their Bible remains uncharted waters for them. I suspect they have seen apocalyptic movies or even heard sermons where Revelation's horrific judgments are portrayed in graphic detail. Mental images of blood rivers, 100-pound hailstones, demonic locusts, global earthquakes, the antichrist, the number 666, and believers being beheaded are enough to give anyone nightmares, particularly if they think there's a chance they might have to endure such a time.

However, I believe this fearful response also has something to do with how they have been taught to view God and His Word. Their preformed image of God seeks to buffer or mute Scripture's portrayal of Him as a God of wrath. "God wouldn't do that to people—He loves them" is not an uncommon reaction. Others' compassionate personalities have a natural aversion to wrath and judgment. This is understandable. But because of this, they end up missing other *comforting* truths found in the Revelation of Jesus Christ.

What has escaped these Christians' notice (or maybe it was never presented to them) is that God "*rescues* us from the wrath to come" (1 Thessalonians 1:10), and that He has "*not destined us for wrath*, but for obtaining salvation through our Lord Jesus Christ (1 Thessalonians 5:9).[2] The context of both these passages concerns the age of the apocalypse and end times. Therefore, the more we know about Bible prophecy, the more hope we have. But never a sense of anxiety or dread. This demonstrates once again that fear is always the enemy of faith.

Actually, this fear-fueled reaction to the end-times narrative more accurately describes what *unbelievers* experience during the tribulation period, in which case it is justifiable and appropriate for them (Revelation 6:16-17).

4. "I really don't see the practical relevance of prophecy to my daily life."

Let's be honest. As humans, we always want to know what's in it for us, don't we? What are the perks? The benefit package? The payoff? This is a natural question, and one that isn't necessarily sinful or selfish. God wants us to internalize and apply His Word. It was He, not us, who said, "All Scripture is...profitable for teaching, for reproof, for correction, for training in righteousness" (2 Timothy 3:16). His words, not ours. So it's a good thing to ask, "What can prophecy do for me?"

And it's here that the adage "Knowledge is power" holds true. When it comes to studying prophecy, that "knowledge power" involves a supernatural enablement from God Himself. Knowing and engaging with prophecy enables you to embrace the truth of God. This influences your thinking, which in turn affects both your decisions and emotions. As you become more familiar with what God says is going to take place on planet Earth, you are able to move forward by faith and, like Noah, realize your purpose and fulfill your destiny!

So what *does* knowing about prophecy do for you?

1. Prophecy helps you understand the times in which you live (1 Chronicles 12:32; Daniel 2:28).

2. Prophecy calms your fears about the future (Matthew 28:20; John 14:1-3,27).

3. Prophecy gives you confidence, courage, and comfort in the present (1 Thessalonians 4:13-18; John 16:33).

4. Prophecy increases your faith in God who's in control of earth's story (Isaiah 40:12-26; Psalm 115:3; Daniel 4:35). Revelation 4 precedes 5–18.

5. Prophecy strengthens your confidence in God's Word (Matthew 5:17-18; 24:35; 2 Timothy 3:16-17; 2 Peter 1:20-21). The Bible is batting a thousand.

6. Prophecy builds expectancy and anticipation for what's coming (Revelation 22:10; Matthew 6:10).

7. Prophecy gives you positive hope in a hopeless world, rescuing you from despair (Titus 2:11-15).

8. Prophecy keeps you centered in an age of doctrinal error, heresy, and apostasy (1 Timothy 4:1; 2 Timothy 3:1-17).

9. Prophecy blesses you as you listen to and obey Scripture's prophetic words (Revelation 1:3).

10. Prophecy motivates you to be urgent about your mission here on earth, not wasting your time on worthless pursuits (Ephesians 5:15-16).

11. Prophecy fuels the fire of your desire to see others know Jesus (2 Corinthians 5:10-13; 6:2).

12. Prophecy imparts a perspective on the temporary nature of suffering (John 16:1-4; Romans 8:18).

13. Prophecy helps you prioritize spiritual things over physical things, living wisely (Psalm 90:10-12; 2 Peter 3:11-13).

14. Prophecy purifies your life as you prepare yourself as Christ's bride (1 John 3:1-3).

15. Prophecy helps you know what to expect as you live for God in an increasingly hostile world (John 15:18-23).

So, again, why should every Christian study Bible prophecy?

- Because it's in the Bible (28 percent of the Bible was prophetic at the time it was written).

- Because of the times in which we live.

- Because of false teaching and misinformation on the subject.

- Because of the huge personal benefits.

When asked by His disciples, "When will these things happen, and what will be the sign of Your coming, and of the end of the age?" (Matthew 24:3), Jesus took time to prophesy many of the events found in the book of Revelation. Then He took their minds back to another ancient prophecy regarding the days of Noah (Matthew 24:1-39). For them (and us), understanding the past is key to making sense of the future and navigating the present.

I encourage you to reject the passivity that prevents many Christians from living with confidence, direction, and hope by engaging in what God says about your future!

God highly values His prophetic Word. And Jesus rebuked both the Pharisees and those disciples who failed to recognize, understand, or heed Bible prophecy regarding Him (Matthew 16:1-4; Luke 24:13-32). It stands to reason that if there are prophecies that have not yet come to pass, then God similarly expects His children today to heed them, *especially* if they may soon be fulfilled.

The Bible was written not simply to be marveled at, but to be understood and obeyed. Admittedly, the meaning of a Bible prophecy is not always immediately discernible at the time it is given or recorded. Many are not understood until the actual time of their fulfillment.

(We'll discuss this more in chapter 5 when we tackle the principles of prophetic interpretation.) But to detour around an entire field of theology just because it doesn't seem directly applicable to our lives demonstrates a shallow spirituality, a lack of hunger for God's Word, or just plain apathy.

I take it you are the kind of disciple who would rather know and grow. If so, turn the page.

Chapter 2

Don't Misread the Signs

The Six Big Mistakes People Make with Prophecy

See to it that no one misleads you.

Matthew 24:4

The world of Bible prophecy is a fascinating field of study, but it is not without its pitfalls. There seems to be a cacophony of noise concerning the end times today. Supposed signs in the heavens, sensationalized headlines, apocalyptic theories, and unfounded predictions have created a perplexing prophetic patchwork, often creating more confusion than clarity. So, how do we navigate through this prophetic haze?

The Perils of Prophecy

Part of the challenge is that along the path of prophecy are hidden land mines, traps that snare you, and stumbling blocks that threaten to trip you up in your quest for God's truth. You need a spiritual mine detector alerting you to potential booby traps. These perils along our path further prevent us from understanding the nature, meaning, and possible fulfillment of Scripture's prophetic truth. Through my experience over the years, I've seen many well-intentioned Christians fall prey to schemes and errors that only further lead away from the path of discovery.

I've identified what I believe to be the Six Big Mistakes people make with Bible prophecy. These act like padlocks, preventing us from entering, understanding, and applying prophecy to our lives.

Mistake 1—Sensationalizing Prophecy

When it comes to prophecy, there is no shortage of sensationalism. Admittedly, the genre does lend itself to a certain degree of hype and hyperbole. Prophecy, by nature, is designed to get our attention, even at times to shock us. Truth about the end times is intended to be a wake-up call. It is a jolt to the nervous system and inherently emotional. Think about it. Apocalyptic Scripture deals with the end of the world, a subject that has fascinated humankind for centuries. In it we see global chaos and calamity. Far from the future utopia for which starry-eyed dreamers hope, according to the Bible, humankind's future is filled with events and seasons that are, well...*sensational*. So yes, there is a degree of the spectacular associated with this subject.

However, when painting a portrait of things to come, some of prophecy's pundits tend to veer off course, sometimes wandering off the map altogether. We saw this back in 1988 with Ed Whisenant's *88 Reasons Why the Rapture Will Be in 1988*. Over four million copies of this pamphlet were sold. We've seen it since then with Y2K, the Mayan apocalypse, and the exaggerated buzz about blood moons. In 2017, another end-times sensation arose regarding an astrological sign in the sky. This celestial alignment, some claimed, was a certain fulfillment of Revelation 12. Turns out it wasn't. Go figure.

So, sensationalism gets our attention. And *over*-sensationalism gets a lot of people's attention. But there's a line between effectively communicating an interesting topic and turning Bible prophecy into a circus sideshow. Like yesteryear's carnival barkers, straw hat and cane in hand, promoting the magnificent claims of their exhibits, we must avoid sounding like those who once promoted the likes of Jo-Jo the Dog-Faced Boy, the Alligator Man, or the Human Pin Cushion.

As a ten-year-old boy, I vividly remember going to the county fair in my hometown of Anderson, South Carolina. Strolling wide-eyed down the midway, popcorn in hand and a pocket full of one-dollar bills, I encountered such a promoter.

"Hey, sonny!" the man yelled, pointing at me. "Have you seen Goliath yet?"

Though I was an unchurched preteen with very little knowledge of the Bible, I did grow up in the South and was aware of the famous giant from Scripture. Upon hearing the man's voice, my attention was temporarily diverted from the corn-dog stand dead ahead. I turned to my left and saw a large tent with a mural painted across the front. On it was portrayed a young boy who looked to be about my age. Standing across a valley from him was a colossal figure with a menacing grin on his face. The oversized man possessed bulging muscles, sported a thick black beard, and held a long spear. The sword hanging from his waist appeared taller than the young boy.

"Just one dollar...four quarters gets you inside the Philistine throne room, young man!" the man out front yelled. His words aroused my boyhood curiosity. I dug into my pockets and produced a crumpled dollar bill, eagerly passing it to the man. He motioned me toward the tent with his cane, and I slowly made my way through the canvas doorway. Once inside, I turned to my right and witnessed a sight so amazing that it stopped me dead in my white Chuck Taylor sneakers. There, sitting on a big, throne-like chair, was the largest human being this freckled-faced kid had ever seen. His huge feet were clad in leather sandals laced up to his calves. A leather tunic, complete with fish-scale armor, covered his chest and ran down to his mid-thighs. On his forearms were protective sheaths. An enormous bronze helmet hung next to him, right beside a steel-tipped spear that seemed ten feet tall.

The giant detected me out of the corner of his eye and motioned me forward.

"Come, little boy," he said with a deep, reverberating voice. "Come closer and see Goliath."

A faint smile appeared through his black-as-night beard, and a muffled laugh exited his throat, the kind you might expect from a giant. Reaching out to grab his spear, he stood up on the slightly raised platform. Up and up he went, and it seemed as if his head would poke through the top of the tent. He was beyond being just tall. He was huge. Broad shouldered. Muscular and mean-looking.

"Well?" he bellowed. "Are you impressed?"

Frozen in shock and amazement, all I could manage was a slow, affirmative nod. Goliath sat back down, took a swig from a chalice, and offered to answer any questions I might have.

"H-h-how tall are you?" I managed to murmur.

"Eight feet tall! What else?"

There was nothing else I could think to ask. I sheepishly exited through the other side of the tent, hoping he wouldn't grab me as I passed by. What had been only a brief visit had felt more like an hour. Once outside in the autumn night air, I exhaled deeply, trying to process what I had just seen. Of course, I knew the giant in the tent wasn't the real Goliath. But something inside me sincerely *wanted* him to be.

My encounter that evening long ago reminds me of some of the messages I hear publicized in the world of prophecy today. There are sensationalist claims of supposed Bible predictions coming true, signs in the sky, world leaders being groomed for apocalyptic roles, and hidden numerical Bible codes. Like my "Goliath," there are usually some similarities or kernels of truth either at the premise of their claims or sprinkled in along the way.

I don't believe it's wrong to promote Bible prophecy, or even reasonably speculate how some of Scripture's end-times claims *could* take place in our lifetime. Speculation is okay, as long as it is communicated properly. However, we have to avoid creating a prophecy circus where unfounded predictions are made and where people's minds and emotions are manipulated. We should always major on what the Bible *does* say and tread cautiously in those areas where it doesn't. And in all our claims, there must be a spirit of integrity, humility, reverence for

God's sovereignty, and a deep respect for the hearer/reader. So watch out, and don't fall for this trap.

Mistake 2—Scoffing at Prophecy

Writing under the inspiration of the Holy Spirit, the apostle Peter prophesied 2000 years ago,

> Know this first of all, that in the last days mockers will come with their mocking, following after their own lusts, and saying, "Where is the promise of His coming? For ever since the fathers fell asleep, all continues just as it was from the beginning of creation." For when they maintain this, it escapes their notice that by the word of God the heavens existed long ago and the earth was formed out of water and by water, through which the world at that time was destroyed, being flooded with water. But by His word the present heavens and earth are being reserved for fire, kept for the day of judgment and destruction of ungodly men (2 Peter 3:3-7).

Scoffers and mockers are nothing new to our faith. From ancient history, Pharaohs and foolish atheists have ridiculed and dismissed the clear truth about God (Exodus 5:2; Psalm 10:4; 14:1). However, here Peter predicts that in the last days, these self-serving mockers will particularly scoff at the prophetic promise of Jesus's return. Jude quotes Peter in his epistle, adding that these same words of warning were spoken by more than one apostle (Jude 17-18). These mockers are energized by their own depraved hearts and sinful desires. They cause division and are worldly minded. Jude says they do not even possess the Spirit of God in them (Jude 19). We see this same attitude reflected in our age today, where many in our world and culture have no fear of God (Psalm 36:1; Romans 3:18). Jude further states that they also "reject authority, and revile angelic majesties" (Jude 8). In other words, such persons stubbornly defy anyone confronting them with absolute truth and biblical morality. They are apostates and gods unto themselves. Satisfying the thoughts and pleasures of their sin nature is their chief pursuit. Therefore, when the uncomfortable prophecy of Christ's return is presented to them, they bristle and belittle such a truth since it threatens to undermine their worldview and undo their self-rule.

It is no surprise that today, the historic beliefs in the blessed hope and the second coming of Jesus Christ are among the most maligned doctrines. Of course, we expect that from the world and from a godless culture. And yet, even within Christendom, some contemporary theological persuasions deny the rapture altogether, spiritualizing most, if not all, of Revelation. This denial and reinterpretation may not mirror the blatant non-Christian mocking of which Peter and the apostles prophesied, but their dismissal of a literal rapture, return, and reign of Jesus has the same end effect. The good news is that if history has taught us anything regarding Scripture, it's that God's prophetic truth always validates itself in time. The mockers are not coming. They have already arrived and set up camp.

Mistake 3—Ignoring Prophecy

It makes sense that one of Satan's greatest strategies would be to distract God's people from a timely, relevant word from Him. In the Old Testament, Israel repeatedly refused to listen to God's prophets (Daniel 9:6; Hosea 9:7; Jeremiah 6:10; 25:4). Whether it was a call to repentance or a prophecy related to a future event, time and time again "they did not listen or incline their ears, but stiffened their necks in order not to listen or take correction" (Jeremiah 17:23).

We see the same principle repeated in the New Testament, when Jesus rebuked the Pharisees for their deliberate refusal to recognize Him as the Messiah:

> The Pharisees and Sadducees came up, and testing Jesus, they asked Him to show them a sign from heaven. But He replied to them, "When it is evening, you say, 'It will be fair weather, for the sky is red.' And in the morning,

'There will be a storm today, for the sky is red and threatening.' Do you know how to discern the appearance of the sky, but cannot discern the signs of the times? An evil and adulterous generation seeks after a sign; and a sign will not be given it, except the sign of Jonah." And He left them and went away (Matthew 16:1-4).

These Jewish religious leaders were looking for miraculous signs, but Jesus directed their attention to *the* sign of the times that was standing right in front of them! In Acts, Peter excoriated those same leaders for their rejection of the prophesied Messiah (Acts 4:8-12). And in the sermon that sealed his execution as the first Christian martyr, Stephen called out Israel's religious leadership to their faces:

> You men who are stiff-necked and uncircumcised in heart and ears are always resisting the Holy Spirit; you are doing just as your fathers did. Which one of the prophets did your fathers not persecute? They killed those who had previously announced the coming of the Righteous One, whose betrayers and murderers you have now become; you who received the law as ordained by angels, and yet did not keep it (Acts 7:51-53).

And with this, they began grinding their teeth together in raging anger against him. Stephen suffered a painful, brutal death by stoning, all because he confronted them with uncomfortable, indicting prophetic truth.

Today, Christians in 65 countries are being persecuted and horrifically slaughtered simply for professing faith in Jesus. We may not suffer a similar fate here in America anytime soon. And it's unlikely the church will stone us for calling out her ignorance and apathy toward the prophetic Scripture. But as we discern the times, we must also be the voices of prophecy to the millions of professing believers in this country. Ignoring prophecy is not only a big mistake. It is also not an option for those who claim to believe the Bible.

Mistake 4—Being Slow to Believe Prophecy

The subject of Bible prophecy has enjoyed a resurgence in recent years, with many books on eschatology achieving bestseller status. Some of these books have little to do with actual prophesied biblical events, but instead address extrabiblical subjects, such as quasi-prophecies, artificial intelligence, extraterrestrials, Illuminati-like global conspiracies, and apocalyptic speculations in general. Even so, it's clear that end-times prophecy is more than a mere blip on the collective consciousness of our nation.

But there is a big difference between believing and *believing*—a difference between mentally assenting or agreeing to something and taking that belief seriously. It's possible to nod our heads in agreement with the Bible's claims about the end times without it ever affecting our lives. We can be presented with the truth and still not quite connect the dots. But Jesus *expects* us to connect the dots, and to *believe*.

Do you recall the account of the two disciples on the road to Emmaus in Luke 24? The resurrected Christ approaches the pair and begins traveling alongside them, though His identity is supernaturally hidden from them (v. 16). Jesus asks them what they are talking about, and they begin rehearsing the recent events in Jerusalem. They tell of this Jesus, "a prophet who was mighty in deed and word in the sight of God" (v. 19), recounts His crucifixion (v. 20), shares their hope that He would be the reigning Messiah (v. 21) and the rumors about Him being alive again (vv. 22-24).

You would think Jesus would commend them for their knowledge and for their desire to believe. But surprisingly, the risen Christ reprimands them:

> He said to them, "O foolish men and slow of heart to believe in all that the prophets have spoken! Was it not necessary for the Christ to suffer these things and to enter into His glory?" Then beginning with Moses and with all the prophets, He explained to them the things concerning Himself in all the Scriptures (vv. 25-27).

Jesus here is decidedly unsympathetic with their inability to understand the Old Testament prophecies concerning Him. He doesn't say, "Well, I can see how you wouldn't quite comprehend all those prophecies about Me. After all, prophecy is so hard to understand. And they were written so long ago. So, hey, no worries, okay?" Instead, He effectively chastises them with, "You *should* have known. You *should* have believed the prophecies!" He then, during their seven-mile journey, walks them through a prophetic overview of the nature and purpose of the Messiah's first coming.

So, it wasn't only the Pharisees who committed serious errors when engaging Bible prophecy. Even Jesus's own disciples failed to fully appreciate the mission and message of His prophesied incarnation. They were slow to believe, perhaps in part due to their preconceived ideas about who the Christ would be and what He would do upon His arrival.

These days, I see a similar hesitancy. There is not only a suspicion about end-times truths but also a reluctance to embrace them. I believe several factors contribute to this.

First, popular thought today dictates that one cannot really know *anything* with certainty. We live in an age where culture asserts that there is no such thing as absolute, objective truth (even though that statement itself is believed to be absolutely true!). To display confidence, especially in matters related to morality, religion, and the Bible, is now viewed as being arrogant or bigoted. Sadly, even within the church, this perspective has gained traction. In many churches, doctrinal certainty and deep conviction are often portrayed as self-righteousness, pride, and even legalism. Paul's declaration, "Knowledge puffs up while love builds up" (1 Corinthians 8:1 NIV) is often cited, as if somehow the two were mutually exclusive.[1] So, they say, "You can't really know anything for sure as it relates to Bible prophecy."

Second, due to the dominance of social media in our lives, everyone today now has a voice, which by itself is a good thing. Unfortunately, everyone thinks their voice carries equal weight and authority, which is *not* a good thing. Simply by gathering enough followers, anyone can be elevated to "expert" status. So, the Christian layperson's blog posts concerning heaven, hell, the Word of God, or same-sex marriage are received with greater weight than the theologian/pastor with a postgraduate degree and 35 years of ministry and study under his belt. This is not at all to say that laypeople cannot lead others in sound biblical truth. It's also not to say that a trained pastor or author can't be wrong concerning a biblical interpretation. However, with the overabundance of ill-equipped, inexperienced (false) teachers saturating media today, it underscores a disturbing trend and reality. People today are responding more to personal opinion and emotional appeal than to the serious study of God's Word. And this leads innocent sheep to embrace unbiblical beliefs and values.

Third, some are hesitant to believe the claims of Bible prophecy because of the sensationalism I mentioned earlier. Some on the fringe of the prophecy world who speculate regarding things like UFOs and global conspiracies are lumped in with pastors and scholars who promote only what Scripture says about the future.

So, when legitimate Bible teachers contend that a) we are living in the last days, b) Jesus's return for the church could come at any moment, and c) it appears we are ramping up toward the fulfillment of Revelation's end-times prophecies, you can understand why many are slow to receive these truths. Or why they reject them outright. Instead, like the noble-minded Bereans, we should be "examining the Scriptures daily to see whether these things" are true (Acts 17:11).

But do we? Does the church today examine and believe, or do we simply emote? As illustrated with Jesus's encounter with Cleopas and his companion, this "slowness to believe" impedes the body of Christ's ability to wholeheartedly embrace biblical teaching and doctrine today, especially as it relates to prophecy and the end times.

Mistake 5—Misinterpreting It and Misleading Others

It is true that some sensationalize Bible prophecy, and either

knowingly or unknowingly misinterpret it through unbiblical speculation. As an unintended consequence, people become put off, confused, or worst of all, deceived. And God does not like it when people
mislead His children. But Scripture tells us that in the last days, we
can expect more of these false teachers to arise from within the church
(1 Timothy 3:1-3; 6:3-5; 2 Timothy 3:1-9; Jude 1-25). Paul wisely
warned the Thessalonian believers about such persons, particularly as
it related to the rapture and the end times.

> Concerning the coming of our Lord Jesus Christ and our
> being gathered to him, we ask you, brothers and sisters,
> not to become easily unsettled or alarmed by the teach-
> ing allegedly from us—whether by a prophecy or by word
> of mouth or by letter—asserting that the day of the Lord
> has already come. Don't let anyone deceive you in any way
> (2 Thessalonians 2:1-3 NIV).

Here, Paul tells us several important things about these false prophets and how they operate. First, they establish themselves as authori-
ties on biblical truth. They quote, misquote, or otherwise cite credible
sources, and by doing so seek to validate themselves as trusted voices in
the arena of faith. Paul's letter to the Thessalonian believers was meant
to refute their claims.

Second, they present their case with confidence, making bold
assertions.

Third, they create more confusion and anxiety than they do faith
and peace, as their claims fly in the face of God's previously revealed
truth found in Scripture. A prime example of this is the way Revelation is viewed. We will cover interpretative methods in more detail in
chapter 5. But if Revelation cannot be interpreted from a normal, literal approach, then it really is anyone's guess as to what it means. And
for Christians, seeking the truth can therefore be both a perplexing
and frustrating dilemma.

When tackling the subject of false teachers in his letter to the

Galatians, Paul held nothing back. He became righteously indignant, even to the point of wishing castration on some of them (Galatians 5:7-12)! The theological issue there was not prophecy but works-based salvation. However, we should never minimalize the significance and impact of any doctrine or area of biblical theology. And eschatology certainly rises up on the plain of Scripture's theological landscape.

Misinterpreting prophecy basically means people say things the Bible doesn't say. They reach conclusions that do not flow from a reasonable understanding of the prophetic Scriptures. And misinterpretation leads to a final huge error people make with Bible prophecy.

Mistake 6—Misapplying It

Misinterpretation of Scripture many times leads to misapplication. This further beguiles the bride of Jesus concerning what it means to walk with God, especially those not familiar with what the Bible actually teaches. There are sensible and proper responses to Bible prophecy already outlined for us in Scripture. But none of them include selling all your possessions, hiding in an underground bunker, or waiting for Christ's return on a remote mountain. For believers, the application of God's prophetic truth never produces panic. It never fosters fear. It never arouses anxiety. On the contrary, in an apocalyptic story written by a personal God, fatalism fades into nothingness. Christians should never dread the prophetic Scriptures or approach the future with apprehension. These reactions arise either from misinterpretation, misunderstanding, or misapplication of what the Bible says concerning the last days. If you've experienced any of these in the past, then either prophecy was miscommunicated to you or you incorrectly received it in your mind and heart.

We will look more specifically at some of the ways prophecy practically impacts our lives in chapters 9 and 10. But for now, know that as with any doctrine, there are both legitimate and erroneous ways to apply them. And eschatology is no exception to that rule. Incorrectly responding to prophecy is a big mistake that must be avoided because it affects the way we live. Fortunately, there are plenty of valid responses.

For example, hope is a huge by-product of engaging the prophetic Scriptures (Titus 2:11-15). So is purity (1 John 3:1-3), security (John 14:1-3,27), confidence (John 16:33), comfort (1 Thessalonians 4:13-18), expectancy (Matthew 6:10; Revelation 22:10), and a life filled with purposeful urgency (Romans 13:11).

Because we are living in the last days of the church age, this is all the more reason Bible prophecy is immensely applicational. God intended for us to know what His Word says—to understand it, believe it, and live our lives in light of it. In fact, it is His desire is that *every believer* read, hear, and take to heart the prophetic word (Revelation 1:3). When studied in its proper context, like the rest of God's written record, prophecy is "profitable for teaching, for reproof, for correction, for training in righteousness" (2 Timothy 3:16). It is an integral part of our maturation in Christ (Ephesians 4:11-16; 2 Timothy 3:16-17; 2 Peter 1:1-3).

As we examine the topography of prophecy, let's be aware of these mistakes and traps that threaten to prevent us from understanding God's Word. Let's take careful steps to avoid the land mines in our pursuit of God's truth. Knowing they exist and identifying them is an essential key to unlocking these end-times mysteries.

The next key turns the lock of discernment.

Chapter 3

Developing Biblical Discernment

Meet the New "Sons of Issachar"

This I pray, that your love may abound still more and more in real knowledge and all discernment.

<small>PHILIPPIANS 1:9</small>

Three not-so-bright fellows were walking through the forest one day when they happened upon a set of tracks. The first one said, "Those are deer tracks." The second one argued, "No, those are elk tracks." Whereupon the third man shook his head, responding, "Both of you idiots are wrong. They're moose tracks."

All three men were still arguing when the train hit them. Clearly, these fictitious men weren't the sharpest knives in the drawer.

What amazes me today is that the things that should be so blaringly obvious seem to be hidden from even the most educated among us. Ours is the most technologically advanced era in all of human history. Thanks to the Internet, the average first-world citizen has more accessible information than all previous generations combined. And the World Wide Web is constantly contracting and expanding, like a breathing universe of data—storing, processing, and computing unimaginable bits of information. Based on 2015 data, it would take you over five years to watch all the videos that travel across the Web every second![1] With currently more than one billion websites, and more than five hundred new ones created every 60 seconds, the amount of information out there is truly staggering.[2] And that smartphone most of us hold in our hands unlocks a portal into what is the equivalent of some 305 *billion* pages of print.[3] That's a library of entertainment, interaction, and knowledge so vast that none of us could possibly absorb a fraction of it in a hundred lifetimes.

And yet, even with unprecedented access to such an excess of knowledge, humankind's lack of real understanding is at a historic high. And nowhere is that more evident than when it comes to discernment. An often-misunderstood word, discernment can be defined simply as "the ability to judge well." Of course, to qualify this, we must also define both what "judge" and "well" mean.

Every person, Christian and atheist, religious and pagan, exercises judgment every day. We make judgments about what food to eat, how to spend our time, whether to speed through a yellow light, or what to browse online. We also make moral judgments—whether to follow our sinful urges or to obey our conscience. And we make moral judgments about others as well. For example, if a serial killer is proven to have brutally murdered a child, virtually everyone would agree he should be judged for his crime. We wouldn't simply let him go free in the name of tolerance or invoke the ever-popular "Who am I to judge?" defense.

This highlights the fact that when it comes to questions involving truth and morality, Christians are often pressured to keep their judgments to themselves. Meanwhile, a depraved culture glories in its self-righteous condemnation of Christ's bride when we declare the mind of God on such issues as homosexuality, abortion, or same-sex marriage. So everybody judges. The only difference is what you appeal to as your standard of judgment: self, society, or Scripture.

Judgment has been redefined in recent years and is now equated with condemnation of someone. Judgment = hatred. Judgment = bigotry. Judgment = self-righteous intolerance. It's a false representation and redefinition of Matthew 7:1—"Do not judge so that you will not be judged." It is the ultimate comeback meant to instantly silence the Christian and his arguments against immorality. Wildly misinterpreted, these words, spoken by Jesus, warned against condemning others for violating the same standards we also violate, as we will also be judged by those standards. Obviously, self-righteous, hypocritical (condemning) judgment is prohibited by God. But making sound judgments about morality is not only allowed, it's even commanded by God (Matthew 7:1-2,6,15-20).

I realize this sounds puritanical in our day, but only because of the moral and spiritual decline of our country. Three contemporary factors contribute to this.

1. The mantra of the age claims, "Only God can judge me." We see this most when people try to justify their immoral or unrighteous lifestyles. Ironically, the behavior supposedly covered by this verbal escape clause is typically already judged by God in Scripture (homosexuality, murder of the unborn). But this is the climate and the spirit of the age that pervades our culture. Christians are condemned for "playing God" (i.e., making moral judgments regarding others' values or behavior), while at the same time, our condemners "play God" by posturing themselves in a judging role over *our* values and behavior.

2. Many high-profile Christians have lived contradictory lifestyles by preaching one thing and living another. Everything from celebrity pastor scandals to prosperity gospel preachers to abuse of power by pedophile priests has combined to stain the character of Christendom in the public eye.

3. Finally, Christians are also capable of making legitimate moral judgments, but with angry hate-filled hearts. The sin nature in believers cannot regulate itself and often

declares God's truth without compassion. Even in our anger against sin, we must leave vengeance to the Lord and give Him room to bring others to repentance (Romans 12:17-21; 2 Peter 3:9). James reminds us that "the anger of man does not achieve the righteousness of God" (1:20). Emotionally as well as theologically, we can easily cross the threshold from righteous zeal to fleshly anger.

Matthew 7 was not a prohibition against making moral judgments about others. Rather, Jesus was telling His disciples not to be hypocritical or self-righteous in these judgments, as the same standard of righteousness will be applied to them for their own behavior.

So, this aspect of discernment (judging) is not the problem; it's the attitude (self-righteous) and the manner (hypocrisy) of judgment that Jesus condemns.[4] Simply declaring what heaven says about sin and sinners is not the same as personally condemning someone, as the judgment does not originate from man but rather from God. Jesus told those gathered in the temple, "Do not judge according to appearance, but judge with righteous judgment" (John 7:24).

And where is this righteous judgment found? According to Christ, it's found in the Word which comes from God, with Jesus Himself being the supreme Judge (John 5:45-47; 8:47; 12:48; Acts 10:42; 17:31; Romans 2:14-16). We're going to put this kind of righteous discernment to use in the next chapter.

"Judging" is something every person does every day regarding personal choices, life decisions, and moral issues. The issue is not judgment but the heart attitude and standard used.

But how can we know whether we have judged correctly? What determines this? Typically, people exercise judgment based on whether it makes them feel good, pleases them, or brings a desired result.

Is there a standard by which all discernment is measured? Is there an absolute, unchanging yardstick of judgment by which all things can be measured?

Some behavior violates both the laws written on our nation's books and the moral conscience laws written on our hearts. Romans 2:14-15 tells us even unsaved people have the moral law of God written in their hearts. And when they consciously suppress this moral knowledge, they then lose the ability to make sound judgment (Romans 1:18-22; 1 Corinthians 2:14).

Look around your world and you'll observe that sound judgment has become about as rare as an Alabama snowstorm in July. Our culture has done to righteous discernment what it has done to decency and other Christian virtues—hijacking them, defying them, denying them, redefining them, and reapplying them to their own values and behavior. As a result, our country (and the world) are in a critical moral and spiritual decline. Though a significant percentage of our country's adults believe we are living in the end times as described by Scripture, few really understand the significance of those prophecies or how they affect their lives.

The Bland Leading the Bland

But this phenomenal lack of biblical judgment isn't unique to the secular world. Many Christians also lack this discernment. I believe we are seeing a huge downgrade of discernment in the contemporary church. So does Pastor John MacArthur, who writes, "The biggest problem in the church today is the absence of discernment. It's a lack of discernment. It's the biggest problem with Christian people, they make bad choices. They accept the wrong thing. They accept the wrong theology. They are prone to the wrong teaching. They're unwise in who they follow, what they listen to, and what they read."[5]

We live in an unprecedented age of access to biblical truth here in our country. In addition to an overabundance of Bibles and churches, we have tens of thousands of Christian books, literature, blogs, websites, speakers, conferences, and Bible studies. It seems that today, every subculture and group has its own special edition of the Scriptures. We have journaling Bibles, a gazillion study Bibles, and about 50 major translations in the English language. It is no surprise then to learn that in America, 87 percent of American households still own a Bible.[6]

Therefore, with all these incredible resources, you'd think American Christians would be the most well-read, knowledgeable, and studious believers imaginable, right?

Not exactly.

According to the Barna Group, though almost 70 percent of teenagers own a Bible, only 3 percent read it daily.[7] Among churchgoing adults, only 19 percent read their Bibles daily, 18 percent never read it, and 14 percent read it about once a week. That's not only embarrassing, it's also very disturbing.

It's like having a neighborhood grocery store with fully stocked shelves but rarely seeing customers take advantage of this abundance. They may eat out once a week, but for the most part, they are content to starve or eat junk food the rest of the time.

So, while running the risk of insulting your spirituality here, allow me to state the obvious. The Bible is God's written revelation to humankind. It's inspired, inerrant, and infallible (2 Peter 1:20-21). It contains everything we need pertaining to faith and godliness (2 Peter 1:3). It is our milk (1 Peter 2:1), our meat (Hebrews 5:14), our water (Ephesians 5:26), and our daily bread (Matthew 4:4). It is our light (Psalm 119:105) and our sword (Hebrews 4:12).

Psalm 19 states that God's Word restores our souls (v. 7), makes us wise (v. 7), gives us joy (v. 8), enlightens our eyes (v. 8), speaks to every age (v. 9), and is to be valued above all other possessions (vv. 10-11). It x-rays our hearts and minds (Hebrews 4:12), makes us holy (John 17:17; Psalm 119:9-11), and abides forever (Psalm 119:89; 1 Peter 1:23).

It's the only book God ever wrote, and He wrote it for us! So, why are Christians neglecting such a treasure of truth? Part of the answer is found by looking back at the first-century church. There, we see a similar spiritual deficiency. In just two short generations following the death, resurrection, and ascension of Jesus, the church had drifted far from its biblical moorings—so much so that she hardly resembled herself. In Jesus's excoriating Revelation messages to the seven churches in Asia Minor, among the things He rebuked them for was not honoring God's truth (Revelation 2:14-16,20). Now, as then, the church is made up of fallible followers who are prone, over time, to fall away from Jesus, losing the hunger and zeal they once had for Him and His Word.

However, considering the current lack of engagement Christians have with the Scriptures, is it any wonder that we consequently lack the discernment to understand and navigate through the confusing times in which we live? Living in the last days and racing toward Revelation, it appears as if Satan has the church right where he wants her, as the bride of Christ has little understanding of this prophetic season.

The tragic irony of this is that at no time in church history has there been a greater need for believers to engage and understand Bible prophecy. The hour demands it. Unfortunately, with biblical illiteracy having gone viral throughout the body of Christ, we find ourselves in a state of unpreparedness.

However, this is in stark contrast to what God wants for His people. I believe this discernment deficiency is the fruit of churches who are more committed to expediency than exposition of the Scriptures. Their members have grown accustomed to a spoon-fed spiritual diet consisting mainly of milk and entertaining, self-help sermonettes. This is a tragic missed opportunity, for studies indicate what attracts people to church most is "sermon content."[8] It was Paul who championed the priority of preaching the Word, uncompromising in an age of ear ticklers (2 Timothy 4:1-5). Part of this preaching involves equipping the church with what God says about future events. Paul told the Thessalonians he did not want them to be uninformed, but rather for them to have clarity, understanding, and hope, *especially* as it related to the end times (1 Thessalonians 4:13).

In light of this, one thing becomes critically clear. We must reverse this trend and become a generation of believers who, like the sons of

Issachar, "understood the times, with knowledge of what [we] should do" (1 Chronicles 12:32).

Not All Discernment Is Discernment

As we observe humanity, it's easy to identify four phases or levels of discernment. Here they are, in ascending order.

Phase 1—Common Discernment

Scripture makes it clear that all humanity, without exception, is born with a basic knowledge of God, exhibited both in creation as well as in conscience (Romans 1:18-20; 2:14-15). This undeniable truth about the Creator's existence, power, divine nature, and His moral law makes humanity inherently accountable to Him. An aspect of what we often call "common grace," this knowledge God gives is encoded within us as a species. Every person naturally understands and discerns that God *is*, and that in our hearts there is written a basic standard of right and wrong. It is common to all humankind, from Los Angeles to Leningrad, Paris to Papua New Guinea, and among every nation, race, tribe, and tongue.

Phase 2—Corrupted Discernment

What we do with that gift of common discernment is up to us. Those who respond positively to it eventually find themselves bowing at the foot of the cross.[9] The rest are hardened, and this helps explain a second level of the discernment experience, one that is incapable of grasping the reality and truth of God. This lower level of understanding is indicative of an unregenerate mind, a characteristic of those Scripture refers to as the "natural man." Paul describes this for us in 1 Corinthians 2:14 (NIV): "The person without the Spirit does not accept the things that come from the Spirit of God but considers them foolishness, and cannot understand them because they [things of the Spirit] are discerned only through the Spirit."

Without a person's spirit being made alive through salvation and the accompanying indwelling and illuminating ministries of the Holy Spirit, the "things of the Spirit" (i.e., spiritual things) are incomprehensible to him. Generally speaking, God's truth evades such people. It sails over their heads. These persons are spiritually dead, therefore we cannot expect them to comprehend the dynamic truths of God any more than a lifeless corpse can be expected to sit up and read Shakespeare. Bear in mind, this corrupted discernment doesn't stem from an absence of intelligence or education, but rather an inability to comprehend divine revelation. Paul is explaining here not a cognitive problem, but a spiritual one.

This, then, is the natural state of humanity apart from Christ. And it clearly explains our culture's depraved condition. But contributing to this corrupted discernment is also a darkening in their understanding. According to Ephesians 4:17-18, when a person hardens their heart toward the inherent knowledge of God, a spiritual darkness (blindness) sets in, leading to a futility in their reasoning. They cannot see truth or reason correctly about spiritual matters because they are blind. This happens because a vast majority of humanity chooses to suppress the evidence of God and His moral law presented to them through creation and conscience. It's a degenerative condition Paul describes in Romans 1:21. Speaking of the willful rejection of truth about God, he says this produces a darkened heart and foolish speculations. Ask a natural man (unsaved) to accept, explain, or understand biblical truths concerning creation, absolute moral law, sexuality, marriage, heaven, hell, salvation, judgment, or prophecy, and he becomes the proverbial blind hog trying to find an acorn. It's a shot in the dark; an almost guaranteed swing and a miss.[10] Without a spiritual rebirth, our thinking is flawed, molded, and enslaved by self and society (2 Corinthians 4:4; Ephesians 2:1-3; Romans 12:1-2).

Therefore, a corrupted discernment is one devoid of spiritual life. It cannot and does not receive the truths found in God's Word.

Phase 3—Casual Discernment

This category of discernment describes many, if not most, professing Christians today. It is personified by those who are exposed to just enough biblical truth to create a false sense of spirituality and understanding. However, their minds have yet to be fully immersed in and transformed by Scripture. As a result, these believers are unable to connect the dots between Scripture and navigating life in a corrupt culture. They struggle, rowing their tiny boats upstream against the strong current of culture. These believers also have very little idea as to what Bible prophecy is, how it works, and what difference it practically makes in their lives. This is tragic, especially since we're living in the age of prophecy!

To be clear, these Christians know right from wrong. They may even love the Lord, occasionally read their Bibles, and live good lives. But they have not been consistently bathed in God's transforming truth over time. It could be that their pastor focuses on "life topics" designed to give believers a more enjoyable life experience. This is not to say that these are not necessary. But along with sermons on having a happy marriage, parenting, dealing with difficult people, and overcoming failure, pastors must also do for their people what Paul did for his. They should help them use the lens of biblical truth to view the world around them. Christians live in a sinful and volatile world. It stands to reason that we should equip them to understand what God says about it.

We live in the context of local, national, and global cultures. Therefore, an important part of a believer's spiritual diet should consist of addressing such questions as: How do I view my world and make sense of it using my Bible? How can I learn to discern the times? And why is that even necessary? How do I interpret my culture? And how should I then live in light of this knowledge? These are some of the critical questions seeking Christians must address. They also must be a part of every pastor's agenda as well. The times demand it, and the Scriptures require it. As long as we remain infants in our thinking, we will never be able to rise above the spiritual naiveté that characterizes much of Christendom.

Phase 4—Consecrated Discernment

Thankfully, not all of Jesus's disciples today are content to wade in the shallow end of the pool. And because you are reading this book, chances are you're one of them. You want more than spiritual Fruit Loops for breakfast. You crave solid food and truth you can really sink your teeth into.

Consecrated discernment is the ability to handle the hard stuff, to eat meat and digest it. This kind of understanding allows you to accurately and confidently read life, culture, the world, morality, and prophecy from God's perspective. Look carefully at what Paul says about this in his first letter to the Corinthians.

> The Spirit searches all things, even the deep things of God. For who knows a person's thoughts except their own spirit within them? In the same way no one knows the thoughts of God except the Spirit of God. What we have received is not the spirit of the world, but the Spirit who is from God, so that we may understand what God has freely given us. This is what we speak, not in words taught us by human wisdom but in words taught by the Spirit, explaining spiritual realities with Spirit-taught words. The person without the Spirit does not accept the things that come from the Spirit of God but considers them foolishness, and cannot understand them because they are discerned only through the Spirit. The person with the Spirit makes judgments about all things, but such a person is not subject to merely human judgments, for,

> "Who has known the mind of the Lord,
>   so as to instruct him?"
> But we have the mind of Christ
> (1 Corinthians 2:10-16 NIV).

Similarly, John wrote,

> You have an anointing from the Holy One, and you all
> know...As for you, the anointing which you received from
> Him abides in you, and you have no need for anyone
> to teach you; but as His anointing teaches you about all
> things, and is true and is not a lie, and just as it has taught
> you, you abide in Him (1 John 2:20,27).

Good news: This "anointing" we have received from the Holy
Spirit comes *standard* with salvation's package. We get it when we get
the Holy Spirit, who indwells us the second we place faith in Jesus
Christ (Romans 8:9; 1 Corinthians 12:13). However, this spiritual
understanding (discernment) is something that is nurtured and developed as we seek God and grow in Him.

At a physical birth, nurses evaluate newborns using what is called
an APGAR score where they check for heart rate, skin tone, breathing,
and so on to confirm that the baby has been born healthy and complete.[11] They also count fingers and toes. Similarly, we were born spiritually healthy and complete in Christ. Growing physically doesn't
mean we add fingers, toes, more brains, or vital organs. It simply
means that these grow in development and that we grow in learning
how to use them. God's design is that we continue to develop spiritually as well (Ephesians 4:13). Hebrews 5:11-14 sheds light on this principle as it relates to discernment:

> Concerning him we have much to say, and it is hard
> to explain, since you have become dull of hearing. For
> though by this time you ought to be teachers, you have
> need again for someone to teach you the elementary prin-
> ciples of the oracles of God, and you have come to need
> milk and not solid food. For everyone who partakes only
> of milk is not accustomed to the word of righteousness,
> for he is an infant. But solid food is for the mature, who

because of practice have their senses trained to discern good and evil.

A baby Christian is not yet able to process the deeper truths of Scripture. And a fleshly Christian has little desire to do so. Both are not "accustomed to the word of righteousness." The Bible is still largely a mystery to them. They aren't used to it or comfortable using it. It feels more like a new pair of dress shoes than a well-worn pair of slippers. Therefore, these Christians prefer a spiritual diet that doesn't require much chewing yet. Because they are babies, they gravitate toward comfortable doctrines, favoring those Christian topics that require minimal study or interaction. They choose milk over meat every time, and thus display their spiritual infancy for all to see.

It's not that there is anything wrong with being a spiritual baby. In fact, it's essential that each of us pass through this stage of development. And we expect certain behavior out of infants. It's no surprise to us when they cry for apparently no reason or soil their diapers. Babies are adorable, but they cannot yet care for or discern for themselves.

John MacArthur says, "A small child will stick almost anything into his mouth, touch anything he can reach, go anywhere he can manage to crawl—with no concept of what is good for him and what is bad, what is helpful and what is dangerous."[12]

In the same way, immature Christians will reach out and consume anything with a "Christian" label on it—book, movie, blog sermon, doctrine. We will talk more about this in the next chapter, but it is alarming how many Christians today follow false teachers, swallow false doctrine, believe claims about heavenly visits, and are duped by sensational prophetic predictions. But that's what children do. We don't expect them to know the difference yet. And we don't expect them to speak full sentences or understand everything that's going on around them.

However, if that child is still wearing diapers and craving baby food when he turns ten, something is very wrong. A lack of physical growth and development cannot be hidden, but inadequate spiritual growth can sometimes be concealed under the cloak of age, status, position, or religiosity. It can also be obscured by knowledge of Bible facts and an ability to "speak the language." We often assume a person who has been a Christian for many years is more mature and wise than they actually are. But according to the passage in Hebrews we just read, this is not always the case. By this point in their spiritual journey, they should have grown up. And yet, they are still exhibiting behavior characteristic of infants, particularly when it comes to discernment. They should be teachers by this time, but instead they remain in spiritual diapers.

Like the psalmist, we should also pray "teach me good discernment and knowledge" (Psalm 119:66) and "give me understanding" (119:125). But God also expects us to pursue these things that contribute to our growth and development as believers. This is natural Christianity. It is abnormal and unnatural for us to remain stunted in our development of discernment. As we saw before, most Christians aren't engaging Scripture regularly, so what does that tell us about the level of discernment among today's Christians?

However, with many mainstream churches focused more on entertaining rather than equipping, what else would we expect?

Developing Discernment

There are two primary Greek words translated as "discernment" in the New Testament: *anakrino,* meaning "to question, examine, or use legal or discerning judgment," and *diakrino*, "to separate, make a distinction, differentiate, pass judgment, judge correctly."[13]

Though a special measure of discriminating judgment is given to some in the church as a supernatural spiritual gift (1 Corinthians 12:10), all believers should mature in this area. True biblical discernment involves more than merely knowing right from wrong. The word "good" we saw in Hebrews 5:14 comes from the Greek word *kalos,* meaning "beautiful, approved, precious, desirable, honorable, praiseworthy, morally good."[14] So, the spiritually maturing Christian is not only developing the ability to distinguish between evil and good, but also making careful judgments between good and better, and between better and best. It is being competent to delineate between the essentials and nonessentials regarding truth and life.

It's like the difference between an untrained musical ear and a professional musician possessing perfect pitch. It's the contrast between a weekend do-it-yourselfer and a seasoned craftsman or carpenter.

This kind of maturing discernment requires *time*. It's not something you get simply by listening to a sermon or reading a book, though both can contribute to growth. Rather, it's a *life skill* that is developed over much time spent in the Word and through life practice ("who because of practice have their senses trained to discern good and evil"—Hebrews 5:14). Over time your spiritual senses are seasoned. This implies repetition and forming habits of using discernment in real-life situations. The word "trained" in Hebrews 5:14 is an athletic term that referred to the discipline exercised in ancient Greek competition. It's also the root word from which we get *gymnasium*.[15] It's the same word Paul used when urging young Timothy to "*discipline* yourself for the purpose of godliness" (1 Timothy 4:7).[16] The idea is that spiritual discernment is similar to an athletic skill. You may have been born with some natural talent, but that will take you only so far. Any successful athlete is one who participates in ongoing training, always striving for excellence and to get better.

So, the more time you invest getting into the Word and letting the Word get into you, the more you naturally acquire discernment. And as we rely on the Holy Spirit in real-life experiences, we are able to better practice this discernment. That's because God's written revelation equips and empowers us to make discriminating judgments about life, relationships, decisions, and morality. Discernment helps free us from the bondage of legalism (Colossians 2:20-23). It provides us with sound decision-making, motivating us toward purity and integrity (Philippians 1:9-11).

Discernment is also essential to understanding and processing Bible prophecy.

The more you grow in discernment, the more you are able to evaluate the times in which we live based on biblical thinking, not personal feelings, opinions, popular thought, or prophetic trends. Everyone sees the times, but only those with biblical discernment can truly *understand* them.

A few years back, I helped Raymond Damadian, the brilliant man who invented the magnetic resonance imaging (MRI) machine, write his story. Dr. Damadian's invention was undoubtedly one of the greatest medical innovations of the twentieth century. The MRI machine safely and accurately scans the human body, revealing things X-rays and CT scans cannot see. Since its conception and development, the MRI has helped save untold millions of lives.

Biblical discernment is like having a spiritual MRI machine in your head, enabling you to see and understand things worldly philosophy and conventional wisdom miss. By using this discernment and paying attention to our culture and world, we can read the age and know what to do as a result. Discernment cuts through the fog, sifting through the white noise often labeled "knowledge" in our culture.

Biblical discernment is a source of wisdom and direction for our lives. It creates a framework and filter through which we interpret the world and reality. Confusion arises when a believer has no real foundation upon which to build a working worldview. Without biblical discernment, life becomes a navigational nightmare. Not only is God's truth and theology confusing, but Bible prophecy is as well. While all truth is God's truth, there is a particular brand of "truth" that humanity and the world offer. Human discernment is largely flawed by sin. And while common sense and rational decision-making can keep one grounded, it takes God's truth to reveal what's real and ultimately important. In this sense, discernment is like a compass. A God-ordained internal GPS, guiding us step-by-step through an understanding of truth and life.

Additionally, those with biblical discernment see past cutesy trends in the church, calling her back to the Bible and the power of the Holy Spirit. Those with biblical discernment are not duped by worldly philosophies or political correctness. They call out hijacked Christian values and the perverting of biblical morality. They spot counterfeit truth when they see it. Cultural values mean very little to those with discerning minds. The only thing they want to know is, "What does the Bible say?"

In Bible prophecy, this discernment is a key that opens the door of understanding. It not only guards us against extrabiblical assertions, but it also guides us into His truth. What we Christians desperately need today is a renewed dedication to the Word of God and a fierce dependence upon the Holy Spirit. Anything less than this will keep us immature, preoccupied, and naïve in a world racing toward judgment. And while the rest of the world argues over what kind of tracks these are, you'll recognize the train of Bible prophecy bearing down on history.

Chapter 4

Spotting Counterfeit Truth

Fake News and False Prophets, Then and Now

Many false prophets will arise and will mislead many.

MATTHEW 24:11

In the Old Testament, God raised up men through whom He spoke divine revelation to His people. Their job was to proclaim His Word and often foretell what would happen in future generations. Many times, prophets confronted and condemned sin among the people of God and their leaders. They brought reform, announced judgment, and predicted the coming of the future Messiah. They were the Lord's representatives, speaking for Him. And that's a pretty big deal.

But along with those prophets, there also arose counterfeits—false prophets. Scripture describes two kinds of false prophets: those who prophesied on behalf of false gods, such as Baal (1 Kings 18), and those who prophesied falsely in the name of the true God, Yahweh. In Ezekiel 13, God spoke through Ezekiel concerning those who were prophesying from their own inspiration while claiming to speak for God (13:1). He describes them as men who are "following their own spirit and have seen nothing" (13:3). They claimed to have been sent by the Lord and yet the Lord had not sent them (13:6). They saw false visions and uttered lying divinations (13:9). For this, God said His hand would be against them and they would have no place in the counsel of His people. He added that their names would be removed from the house of Israel and that they would not reenter the land following the Babylonian captivity (13:9). The reason for this punishment is that they had lied, misrepresented God, and misled God's people (13:10).

Similarly, God spoke to Jeremiah, declaring,

> This is what the LORD Almighty says:
> "Do not listen to what the prophets are prophesying
>   to you;
>   they fill you with false hopes.
> They speak visions from their own minds,
>   not from the mouth of the LORD" (Jeremiah 23:16 NIV).

These men were pretenders, fakes, and counterfeit communicators. Conversely, one of the characteristics of a genuine Old Testament prophet is that when he predicted future events, they always came to pass exactly as he said they would. Anyone claiming to be a prophet whose prophecy did not come true was subject to a public death by stoning.[1] The Old Testament tells the stories of several such false prophets.[2]

Throughout Scripture we learn that God takes it very seriously when someone claims to be a prophet or to speak for Him.

When we come to the New Testament, we find not only warnings concerning false prophets but also examples of them. During the last week of His earthly ministry, Jesus prophesied that the Jewish temple in Jerusalem would be utterly destroyed. In response to this devastating news, the disciples asked him, "Tell us, when will these things happen, and what will be the sign of Your coming, and of the end of the age?" (Matthew 24:1-3).

Jesus then launches into a description of the end times and the last days of planet Earth. He begins by saying, "See to it that no one misleads you. For many will come in My name saying, 'I am the Christ,' and will mislead many" (24:4-5). A few verses later He prophesies, "Many false prophets will arise and will mislead many" (24:11). Later, in the same conversation, He tells them, "For false Christs and false prophets will arise and will show great signs and wonders so as to mislead, if possible, even the elect. Behold, I have told you in advance" (24:24-25).

While these words of Jesus have their ultimate fulfillment during the tribulation described in Revelation, they do not exclude the multitudes of false prophets and false messiahs that have dotted the landscape of history the past 2,000 years. The three characteristics of these end-times false prophets identified by Jesus are (1) they will mislead many; (2) they will make great claims; and (3) they will perform convincing signs and wonders.

But this was not the first time Christ had spoken about these people. Earlier, in Matthew 7, Jesus warned His disciples,

> Beware of the false prophets, who come to you in sheep's clothing, but inwardly are ravenous wolves. You will know them by their fruits. Grapes are not gathered from thorn bushes nor figs from thistles, are they? So every good tree bears good fruit, but the bad tree bears bad fruit. A good tree cannot produce bad fruit, nor can a bad tree produce good fruit. Every tree that does not bear good fruit is cut down and thrown into the fire. So then, you will know them by their fruits (vv. 15-20).

First-Century "Fake News"

It didn't take long after the church began for false teaching to begin infiltrating the Christian community. Keep in mind, there were no Bibles for believers to consult, only the verbal revelation, and eventually the letters, sent from the apostles. Of course, those letters became the bulk of the New Testament. So, when someone arose from within the church claiming to have a "word" from God or from Paul, this was sometimes difficult to dispute. And that is exactly why Paul warned the Thessalonians of this very thing (2 Thessalonians 2:1-3).

Evidently, some in the Thessalonian church had claimed to receive direct revelation from God concerning the day of the Lord. Knowing that Paul had authority and influence in the Thessalonian believers' lives, these men also piggybacked on the apostle's credibility in order to manipulate and mislead the Christians there.

But the Thessalonian church wasn't the only faith community to suffer from these false teachers. Paul had previously prophesied that this would happen. After his ministry with the Ephesian church came to an end, Paul gathered with the church elders for a tearful farewell, during which he warned them,

> Be on guard for yourselves and for all the flock, among which the Holy Spirit has made you overseers, to shepherd the church of God which He purchased with His own blood. I know that after my departure savage wolves will come in among you, not sparing the flock; and from among your own selves men will arise, speaking perverse things, to draw away the disciples after them. Therefore be on the alert, remembering that night and day for a period of three years I did not cease to admonish each one with tears (Acts 20:28-31).

Paul had served the Ephesian believers with humility and integrity amid much opposition (20:19).[3] Through his teaching ministry, he had declared the whole counsel of God to them (20:20-21,27). He did this in the assembly as well as in small house group gatherings (20:20). Paul didn't simply "start churches"; he established communities of faith, grounding them in God's truth, and then leaving them in the hands of capable pastors and elders. As their founding pastor, he was under divine obligation to teach them all he could while he was with them. But eventually, the time came when his deployment to Ephesus was over (20:24-25).

However, Paul was also keenly aware of three unchangeable realities regarding the church: (1) the selfish nature of the human heart,

(2) the deceptiveness of Satan, and (3) the need to guard the purity of God's truth. These "wolves" of which he warned would appear both from within the church and from outside of it (20:29-30), and their scheme would be to steal away disciples for themselves. His counsel to those elders was to "be on guard for yourselves and for all the flock" and to "be on the alert" (20:28,31).

Sadly, his prophetic words would come true. In his letters to young pastor Timothy, Paul was forced to address such men directly and by name (1 Timothy 1:3-4,20; 2 Timothy 4:14). It makes me wonder if pastors and elders in today's churches have this attitude of being on the alert for false teaching. Do they see themselves as guardians of the truth or merely as board members and administrators of a business-based ministry? I suspect we would see fewer doctrinal aberrations and less false teaching in the church today if more leaders took this responsibility more seriously.

But the infiltration of doctrinal error didn't stop with the Ephesian church. Others would also fall under the attack of false teaching and attempts to undermine Paul's apostolic authority and divine truth previously revealed. Paul dealt with similar struggles with several other New Testament churches. From his letters to these churches, we can piece together a composite portrait concerning what some of these false teachers and their teaching looked like.

Foxes in the Henhouse

There are two primary ways to spot false teachers and their teaching. One is by looking at how they manifested themselves in the New Testament and how Paul responded to them. The second way is to ask some specific diagnostic questions that enable us to identify them. In the rest of this chapter, we will look at both of those methods.

False teachers don't kick in the church door, they walk through it. They establish themselves as trusted leaders, and then they begin influencing other believers. This is what happened to the first-century church, and it inspired Paul to address the issue in those churches he

believed were being threatened. Through looking at their influence
and Paul's response, see if you can pick up some indicators of how
Satan and his servants still operate today.

The Roman Church

The church at Rome was doing well in obedience to the Lord, but
Paul warned them to keep their eyes "on those who cause dissensions
and hindrances" contrary to apostolic teaching (Romans 16:17-20).[4]
The word "hindrance" here means a "snare" or "trap," from which we
get our word *scandal*. Paul is saying, "Watch out for scandalous people who set truth traps." He counseled Roman believers to turn away
from such men, because with "their smooth and flattering speech they
deceive the hearts of the unsuspecting" (16:18).

The Corinthian Church

Most of the false teachers Paul encountered were Judaizers—Jews
previously introduced to the Christian faith, but who also promoted
salvation as a partnership of faith plus obedience to Old Testament
Law. They saw Christianity as a threat to their old way of relating to
God and were not willing to accept the simplicity of the New Covenant. Thus they clung tightly to their Jewish laws and traditions.[5]

These Corinthian false teachers sought to discredit Paul (2 Corinthians 1:12–2:4; 11:1-12). They attacked his ministry, message, character,
and his motivations (1 Corinthians 2:1-5; 3:1-9; 4:1-5; 2 Corinthians
11:5-12). Character assassination is still a favorite tool of the ungodly
today.

His patience having run out, Paul exposes these men as "false apostles, deceitful workers, disguising themselves as apostles of Christ"
(2 Corinthians 11:13). Then he drops the hammer by insinuating that
they are servants of Satan! For "even Satan disguises himself as an
angel of light. Therefore it is not surprising if his servants also dis-
guise themselves as servants of righteousness" (2 Corinthians 11:14-
15).[6] Paul was passionate about preserving the integrity of the gospel.

He didn't care whose feelings he hurt as long as the purity of the faith was maintained.

The Church at Galatia

Paul reserved his most scorching condemnation for the Galatian Judaizers and deals directly with these men. Specifically, he declares that adding anything to Christ's finished work on the cross is nothing less than a different gospel and a distortion of God's truth (Galatians 1:6-7). Anyone who propagates such a gospel "is to be accursed," meaning damned eternally (1:8).[7] And this holds true even if such teaching were to come from an angel. Paul does not mince words when describing those who oppose sound doctrine, plainly calling them "false brethren" (2:4).[8]

The Church at Ephesus

Paul addressed the subject of false teachers in his letters to young Timothy, who pastored the Ephesian church. First and 2 Timothy are filled with a fervency for scriptural teaching and sound doctrine (1 Timothy 1:1-11,18-20; 3:2-3; 4:6-8,13-16; 6:3-5,13-15,20-21; 2 Timothy 1:13-14; 2:1-2,14-21; 3:1-9,13-17; 4:1-5,13). The false teachers at Ephesus were promoting strange doctrines—myths, genealogies, and speculating about the truth (1 Timothy 1:3-4). Though they thought of themselves as teachers, they did not understand what they were talking about. And yet, they spoke with confidence (1 Timothy 1:6-7). Paul labeled their actions as blasphemous (1:2). Their consciences were seared, and they promoted legalism, which Paul calls a "doctrine of demons" (4:1-3). Theirs was not a doctrine conforming to godliness or to Jesus's words (6:3). Like many bogus Bible teachers today, Paul says these men were full of hot air, blowing smoke, and enamored with themselves. They had a morbid interest in controversial questions and disputes about words (6:4). Their hearts were depraved and their minds were deprived of the truth. They thought ministry was merely a means of financial gain (6:5). And they loved to argue (2 Timothy 2:14).

He compares their toxic talk to "gangrene"—empty, ungodly chatter only leading to further ungodliness (2 Timothy 2:16-18). Their unfounded speculations were foolish and ignorant, and only produced quarreling and anger (2:23). In reality, they loved only themselves and the sounds of their own voices, publicly portraying themselves as godly (3:1-5). They preyed on the weak and were masters at manipulation (3:6). And they still had not come to the knowledge of God's truth (3:7).

Paul states that this false teacher phenomenon will get worse in the last days (2 Timothy 3:13; 2 Thessalonians 2:3-4,11). He prophesies that these spurious teachers will enjoy immense popularity among religious crowds. Instead of preaching the Word and sound doctrine, they will teach self-pleasing myths in order to make their audiences feel good (2 Timothy 4:3-4). The itch for entertaining messages will be scratched by the deceptive claws of these wool-clad wolves.

The Church at Philippi

Paul was inspired to warn these believers to be aware of anyone promoting human works as a necessary component of salvation. He labeled them as "evil workers" and "the false circumcision," and even referred to them as "dogs" (Philippians 3:1-3).[9] They trusted in their own works more than Jesus's provision on the cross. Their deceptive influence deeply saddened Paul's heart (Philippians 3:18-19).

The Church at Colossae

One of Paul's battles in the church at Colossae was with what would later be known as Gnosticism. This belief views matter as evil but God (spirit) as good. Therefore, anything done in the body, they assert, is not inherently evil, but only what is in the spirit. Gnosticism comes from the Greek word *gnosis*, which means "knowledge." The Gnostics claimed to possess a higher plane of knowledge that must be attained in order for salvation to be genuine. They believed that Jesus, having come in the flesh, was merely an *emanation* from God, and therefore not fully divine. This clearly contradicts the rest of Scripture

(John 1:14,18; 2 John 7). Paul counteracted this religious philosophy by emphatically declaring that Jesus was the "image of the invisible God" (Colossians 1:15). As God, Christ had "created all things" and all things "were created through Him and for Him" (1:16). Paul adds that it was through Jesus's *fleshly body* that our redemption was accomplished (1:22). He proclaims Christ as being eternal and the sustainer of the universe, and yes, *fully God* (1:17-19).

Other false teachers there promoted the worship of angels and their own patented brand of legalism, requiring circumcision for salvation. They also required abstinence from certain foods and strict adherence to Jewish holy days. And finally, they taught that asceticism (self-denial) was essential to being wise and religious (Colossians 2:11,16-23; 3:11).

Paul corrects the Colossians' thinking by exposing the futility of such bad theology. Jesus needs no contribution from us regarding salvation. We, on the other hand, desperately need His provision of grace (Ephesians 2:8-10).

The Church at Thessalonica

The church of Thessalonica had received false information about the coming of the Lord and the tribulation (1 Thessalonians 4:13-18; 2 Thessalonians 2:1-4). Paul calmed their spirits and set their minds at ease by straightening out their understanding of eschatology and the end times. God's truth is always the antidote to the poisonous lies of false teachers.

The Church at Crete

You may not have heard much talk about this church. They didn't get their own Pauline letter, but did indirectly through their pastor, Titus.[10] Like other New Testament churches, the church at Crete came under attack from false teachers and their lies. Ironically, the Cretan people themselves had developed a reputation for lying, so much so that to "play the Cretan" became synonymous with lying.[11] Paul played off this imagery in his review of the Judaizers, referring to them as "empty talkers and deceivers" (Titus 1:10). They were upsetting entire families with their false teaching, just to make money (1:11). They propagated Jewish myths and man-made rules, damning evidence of their departure from the truth (1:14).

Paul tells Titus to exhort the church in sound doctrine and to refute all those who contradict it (1:9). This was so that they might repent and return to a sound faith (1:9-14). They "profess to know God but by their deeds they deny Him, being detestable and disobedient and worthless for any good deed" (1:16).

Paul encouraged Titus to speak to the church "the things which are fitting for sound doctrine" (2:1).

Christians Scattered in Asia Minor

Peter's epistles were written to believers dispersed throughout Asia Minor (modern-day Turkey). In his second letter, he reveals the characteristics of false teachers and their counterfeit creeds. These men arise from within the church, secretly introducing destructive heresies, and by doing so deny Christ. They are full of sensuality and greed and are masters at exploiting others with their speaking abilities. Even so, Peter adds, a certain judgment is coming for them (2 Peter 2:1-3).

He describes them as indulging the flesh, despising authority, and being brazen in their teachings. They are strong-willed and have no reverence for the power or authority of angels (2:10-11). They sin openly with adultery, enticing unstable believers (2:14). Hell is reserved for such people (2:17). Peter concludes that it would've been better for them to have never known the truth than having known it, to then turn away from it (2:21). They are imposters and fakes.

1 John

The Beloved Disciple makes it clear that we are living in the "last hour" or the "last days" (the period between Jesus's first and second comings (1 John 2:18).[12] And though he affirms that one called "antichrist" will come, he also insists that many other antichrists had already arisen during that time. Today, we are seeing a surge of apostasy in the church, as false teachers have greatly increased within Christendom.[13] These "antichrist teachers," John says, are proof we are living in the last hour. They not only leave the faithful but also the faith itself (1 John 2:19, 23). They are liars and deceivers (2:22,26). And the way to detect these lying spirits, John says, is to test them against God's revelation of truth (4:1-3).

Jude

The entire book of Jude, with only 25 verses, is devoted to defending the faith against false teachers and their teaching.[14] In his letter to those he describes as the "called," "beloved," and "kept for Jesus Christ" (v. 1), Jude describes "certain persons" who "crept in unnoticed," either a reference to their deceptive skills or to a lack of discernment in the church—or both (vv. 3-4). Jude characterizes these peddlers in the following way:

- They have no restraint with regard to their sexual urges (vv. 4,8,10).

- They are dreamers, meaning they either live in a mental fantasy world or appeal to dreams and visions as the source of their authority (v. 8).[15]

- They reject authority and accountability (v. 8).

- They have no respect for angelic majesties (v. 8).[16]

- They're very bad at theology and very good at immorality (vv. 10-11).

- They reject God's ways, like Cain (v. 11).[17]

- They compromise themselves for the sake of money (v. 11).[18] They are prophets for profit.

- They rebel against God-ordained leadership (v. 11).[19]

- They are "hidden reefs" in the church, self-planted to shipwreck the faith of others (v. 12).[20] They're like Satan's secret agents.

- They're "clouds without water," or big talkers that promise much but deliver nothing of spiritual substance (v. 12). Unlike those grounded in the truth, these clouds are "carried along by winds" of false doctrine.

- They're "autumn trees without fruit, doubly dead, uprooted" (v. 12). They have no depth, bear no real fruit, and have no lasting power.

- They're "wild waves of the sea, casting up their own shame like foam" (v. 13). Their ministries are more emotion and show than Spirit and power.

- They're "wandering stars" (v. 13). Like a falling star, they are nothing more than meteoric flashes of light that soon burn out.

Does this sound like some of today's false teachers?

- Then Jude adds that they will burn in hell and their destiny is damnation (vv. 13-15).[21]

- These false teachers are also labeled as "grumblers" who find fault in others (v. 16).

- They follow after their own controlling desires or lusts (v. 16). All they do is motivated by self.

- They "speak arrogantly, flattering people for the sake of gaining an advantage" (v. 16). Their presentations are enticing and persuasive, yet deceptive. They may be eloquent and spiritual sounding. They tell you things that make you like them, while simultaneously making you feel good about yourself. They are all about self-empowerment and building up your self-esteem.

- Jude quotes Paul's warning in 2 Timothy 3:1 that "in the last days difficult times will come" and men will mock God and His truth, exhibiting their own ungodly desires (v. 18).
- They cause divisions in the body of Christ (v. 19).
- They are worldly-minded (v. 19).
- They may speak about Jesus, but they do not possess the Holy Spirit (v. 19).

That they are not truly saved is one of the most frightening things about these counterfeit teachers. They call Jesus "Lord" and even prophesy in His name, yet Christ does not know them or claim them. Instead, He will cast them out of His presence (Matthew 7:21-23). Like their true master, though, they are skilled at disguising themselves as "angels of light" (2 Corinthians 11:13-15).

But it doesn't end there. Like a lingering virus, pseudo-prophets kept infecting the church with their heretical teachings and lifestyles into the end of the first century. In Revelation 2–3, we still see churches being threatened by these errant teachers. Jesus commends the Ephesian church for putting to the test those who falsely claimed to be apostles (Revelation 2:2). But following His rebuke of that church's lost love for Him, He applauds their hatred for the "deeds of the Nicolaitans," an immoral sect that twisted God's grace, allowing themselves to engage in sexual immorality (Revelation 2:6).[22]

The church at Pergamum permitted the "teaching of Balaam" as well as the ways of the Nicolaitans (Revelation 2:14-15). The church at Thyatira "tolerated the woman Jezebel, who calls herself a prophetess" (Revelation 2:20). She, too, led the church into sexual sins. And the church at Sardis had also those who "soiled their garments," a likely reference to apostate teaching and practices.[23]

So clearly false prophets were a real first-century phenomenon, and through the apostles' letters to the churches, we can better know how to identify them and be fully prepared for them.

Spotting Today's Counterfeits

It would be too easy to list a rogues' gallery of false teachers that are infiltrating the church today with their slick philosophies. Their names are well known and their multi-million-dollar ministries well funded. But they are ambassadors of another gospel, drawing their truth from a mash-up of the Bible, self-help philosophy, the power of positive thinking, and occasionally some good old-fashioned voodoo thrown in. So rather than name names, it would be more beneficial to teach you how to spot them yourself.

Therefore, is there a test we can administer to these pastors, teachers, authors, speakers, bloggers, artists, musicians, and performers who are in positions of spiritual leadership? What questions should we ask? And can any professing Christian make this call or is it limited only to certain kinds of believers? The answer to that last question is yes and no. Every authentic Christian possesses the Holy Spirit, the mind of Christ, and His "anointing" (John 14:26; 16:13; Romans 8:9,16; 1 Corinthians 2:6-16; 1 John 2:20,27). Because of this, any believer can discern basic truth and error. However, as we have learned, mature discernment is a life-skill developed over time, requiring a depth of biblical understanding. Since the majority of the church today isn't engaging God's Word regularly or deeply, millions of Christians are falling prey to false teachers and their teaching.

The key to separating truth from error is found in the process of biblical knowledge, discernment, and maturity. Your goal is to let Scripture enlighten you regarding what God says are the often blaring, but sometimes very subtle, characteristics of modern-day Nicolases and Jezebels. It's important that we are not naïve, blindly accepting every preacher, teacher, author, lecturer, apologist, and pastor promoted by a denomination, church, organization, or Christian publisher. Instead, we must examine their teachings. We are not called to judge the motivations of someone's heart. Nor are we able to. Discernment is not a gateway to becoming self-righteous or condescending toward anyone. Discernment is a statement of the truth, not a judgment of the heart. And yet, we dare not overswing the pendulum in the opposite direction and refuse to embrace our responsibility to God and His truth.

Allow the words of Jesus, Paul, and John to give you the keys to begin unlocking these doors of discernment. Jesus prophesied, "You will know them by their fruits" (Matthew 7:20). Paul warned, "Be on the alert" (Acts 20:31). And John exhorted us to "test the spirits" (1 John 4:1).

"I Coulda Been a Contender"

False teachers and their damnable heresies were a real threat to the doctrinal purity and spiritual growth of first-century Christians. No church, no matter how large, well-funded, or well-intentioned, is immune from the potential danger of compromising the purity and power of God's written revelation.

Obviously not every false prophet or false teacher distorts Scripture the same way. Whether the person is ego-driven, seeking celebrity status, courting a large following, seeking financial gain, or merely trying to help someone but are themselves mistaught and misled, one common denominator runs through all of them like a thread through a beaded necklace: They are all in error.

James's admonition rings true here, "Let not many of you become teachers, my brethren, knowing that as such we will incur a stricter judgment" (James 3:1). We are not to cause unnecessary division in the body of Christ by splitting hairs over every truth found in Scripture. And yet, we are called to separate truth from error, and to "accurately handle the word of truth" (2 Timothy 2:15). We are also called to reject those who defy, deny, or redefine "the faith which was once for all handed down to the saints" (Jude 3).

With that in mind, here are some diagnostic questions that will help you discern whether a particular teaching is biblical and whether the teacher is a true shepherd or a wolf in sheep's clothing and thus a false prophet.

- What do they believe about Jesus Christ? Is He fully God, 100 percent deity? Is He fully man, yet without sin? Is He the Christ described in Scripture or an upgraded, enlightened, hip overhaul of an outdated Messiah for a new generation?

- Did Christ make a substitutionary atonement while on the cross?

- Was He physically raised from the dead on the third day?

- How do they believe a person is saved? Is it by grace alone through faith alone in Christ alone? Or do they add *anything* else to this experience?

- In their theology, are all people eventually going to heaven or only those who place faith exclusively in Jesus?

- What do they believe about the Bible? Is it inerrant and infallible, not only in its general teachings but also down to the accuracy of each word? Do they believe any part of the Bible is irrelevant or no longer true?

- Do they modify, revise, or redefine historic doctrines, beliefs, and morals clearly taught in Scripture?

- Do they promote a new belief or spiritual principles not firmly rooted and grounded in the Bible?

- Can what they teach be supported by Scripture?

- Do they explain Scripture or merely communicate "life truth"?

- Are they accountable? How do they respond to criticism and rebuke (Matthew 15:12-14)?

- Do their message and ministry promote Christlikeness or simply more followers of themselves?

- Do they talk more about money than about Jesus and His Word? Are they lining their pockets and padding their bank accounts with money from God's people (2 Corinthians 2:17; 1 Timothy 3:3)?

- Do their own egos, fame, and celebrity status overshadow Jesus and His Word?

- Do they live a hypocritical lifestyle (1 Timothy 4:16; 2 Timothy 3:5)?

- Does their teaching make you feel better about yourself or more consumed by a passion for Jesus?

- Always ask, "What does the Bible say?"

Some of these diagnostic questions are concrete, while others carry an element of subjectivity. But they all require discernment. Be on the alert for those whose egos eclipse the Word of God, whose platform and celebrity status overshadow the "Jesus" they claim to know. Is their presentation greater than the truth they present? View with great skepticism those who offer a new kind of Christianity. Be wary of men and women who question historic doctrines of the faith in order to accommodate postmodern beliefs, morals, and values.

These people are convincing. They are really good at what they do. That's how they got to be where they are. But they're not real. They are merely well-groomed imitations.

They talk about Jesus. They even say "in Jesus's name" a lot. They use Bibles. They are gifted communicators. They act nice. They make you laugh. They may actually do some good and honorable things. They appear so genuine and sincere. However, none of these things qualify a person to speak for God.

According to Jesus, wolves don't show up in their natural clothing. Rather, they appear as sheep in order to appeal to sheep and eventually fleece them.

Satan hasn't given up his agenda and strategy of diluting and destroying Christians and God's church. He is still prowling around seeking someone to devour (1 Peter 5:8). And his servants are the ones doing his bidding.

The signs of a first-century false prophet are the same today. Like those who troubled Paul, today's sinister charlatans are their spiritual descendants. Then, as now, they are con artists. Impostors. Phonies. Pretenders. Quacks. Snake-oil salesmen. A false teacher ultimately wants what his master once wanted in heaven—power and worship. Whether he or she admits it with their lips, their lifestyle and teaching seek glory only for themselves.

In conclusion, the following three words will help you as you face a world filled with false teaching.

1. *Beware*—Jesus says to watch out for false prophets (Matthew 7:15). Avoid them as you would a land mine and tell others about them. They are not harmless, but enemies of the cross (Matthew 23:15; Philippians 3:18-19). And remember, your greatest radar detector is your developing biblical discernment.

2. *Test*—Ask questions of teachers, pastors, authors, and bloggers to see if they are of God or in error. Does what they are saying square with Scripture? Dive into your own Bible and let God's Word guide you (Acts 17:11; 1 John 4:1).

3. *Contend*—It's not just your pastor's job to protect the integrity of God's truth in the church. It's yours as well. Sometimes God will call you to confront the fake news these teachers promote so you can protect your fellow believers. You must wrestle with the forces of darkness to preserve the purity of the faith. God's truth has been entrusted to you. If you don't do battle with Satan's lies through his counterfeit messengers, who will?

Sound doctrine is not a secondary issue; it's the essence of our faith. What we believe about Jesus and what His Word says is of paramount importance and cannot be underestimated. Throughout the New Testament, God exalts His truth to a high and honored position in the church. As Jesus's bride, we are guardians of that truth and tasked with the mission of contending for it in the midst of a crooked and perverse generation.

Chapter 5

Cracking the Bible Code

Proven Principles of Prophetic Interpretation

Be diligent to present yourself approved to God
as a workman who does not need to be ashamed,
accurately handling the word of truth.

2 TIMOTHY 2:15

When my sons were young, we took a family trip to historic Williamsburg, Virginia. One of the attractions there is a huge maze made up of six-foot-tall bushes located behind the governor's palace. The challenge is to find your way through the confusing pathways and eventually reach the center of the maze. I challenged my sons to see if they could beat me to the center. After 15 minutes or so of meandering blindly through the leafy labyrinth, I finally arrived at the center of the large maze. To my surprise, I discovered my four-year-old son standing there waiting on me. Truly *amazed* that he had navigated through this life-sized puzzle ahead of me, I asked, "Son, how in the world did you get here before I did?"

"It was easy, Dad," he replied matter-of-factly. "I just walked through the bushes."

Little cheater.

What my son did at Williamsburg that day is what many attempt to do with Bible prophecy—look for shortcuts and methods to fast-track their way to the center of the prophetic maze. But while prophecy does require a good amount of time and study, it is not an unsolvable puzzle, though it appears that way sometimes.

Prophecy *reveals* God's truth; it doesn't hide it from us. The word *revelation* literally means "to unveil, reveal, or uncover." Yes, a certain amount of biblical training is required, as with other areas of theology. And that equipping is essential as it guards us from faulty conclusions about God's future agenda. But perhaps no other genre of Scripture is so misinterpreted and misunderstood as Bible prophecy. One reason for this is that a number of questionable methods that have recently gained popularity produce more confusion than clarity. It seems that, when attempting to make sense of the end times, almost any approach is acceptable. But while all roads may have led to Rome, not all interpretive methods lead to a trustworthy interpretation of Bible prophecy.

Untrustworthy Means of Interpretation

Here are some of these bogus methods to watch out for.

Numerology

Yes, there are numbers in the Bible. We get it. Some numbers have significance while others do not. Some are repeated in both the Old and New Testaments. Israel spent 40 years wandering in the wilderness. The rain in Noah's flood lasted 40 days and 40 nights. Jesus was tempted in the wilderness for 40 days, and He taught His disciples for 40 days following His resurrection. Other repeated numbers include 4, 7, and 12.

But another way numbers are examined is through what is known as *Gematria*, an ancient Jewish method used to find meanings through the letters of the Hebrew alphabet. Each Hebrew letter carries a specific numerical equivalent. When you convert someone's name into Hebrew, you can assign a number to that name. Some have used this method in trying to determine the identity of the antichrist (666), applying it to everyone from Prince Charles to Bill Clinton to Barack Obama. Obviously, one of the problems with using Gematria as an interpretive method is that the numerical conversion can ultimately apply to multiple persons. This doesn't inspire a confident interpretation of prophetic Scripture. Numbers do have meaning in prophecy, but interpreting Revelation using mathematics isn't a last days' Rosetta stone.

The Jewish Feasts

Undoubtedly, there is spiritual significance in the Jewish feasts of the Old Testament. Jesus was crucified for our sins on the day of preparation for Sabbath, during the celebration of Passover (John 18:28; 19:14). The church was begun on the day of Pentecost (Feast of Weeks). Some today believe the Jewish Feast of Trumpets or Rosh Hashana (Leviticus 23:24; Numbers 29:1-6) is a foreshadowing of the rapture of the church (cf. "the last trumpet" in 1 Corinthians 15:52). But as partakers of a new covenant, Christians do not celebrate Jewish feasts, which were mere "shadows" representing the "substance" (Christ) that was to come (Colossians 2:16-17). Passover was only for Jews under the old covenant. Jesus and His cross, commemorated in the Lord's Supper, are far superior to the rituals and celebrations that are now rendered unnecessary under His new covenant. So, though they are a part of a historic foreshadowing of Christ and His work, the Jewish feasts are not the template through which we predict the coming of the Lord.

Newspaper Exegesis

This misguided method consists of tracking the headlines and then running to the Bible to see if you can fit the event into a prophetic passage or timeline. Although there are certainly stage-setting events and developments that appear to relate to coming prophetic fulfillment, we must be cautious and not assign too much importance to every major geopolitical happening. Too often, when something noteworthy occurs that captivates the world's attention, we mistakenly assume this must somehow be a revelation of unfolding prophecy.

Not long ago a well-meaning gentleman told me he believed President Donald Trump was a divinely appointed forerunner who would somehow usher in the rapture of the church. He came to this conclusion based upon seeing the president's last name in 1 Thessalonians 4:16—"For the Lord himself shall descend from heaven with a shout, with the voice of the archangel, and with *the trump of God*: and the dead in Christ shall rise first" (KJV). Of course, it didn't matter that virtually every other Bible translation renders the word as "trumpet," not "trump." The second reason for his interpretation was that President Trump's middle name is John. And since John the Baptist prepared the way for Jesus's first coming, President Trump would somehow do the same for His return.

The problem with this kind of reckless reasoning is that it ignores actual meanings of words in Scripture. "Trump" means a trumpet, not a man called Trump.[1] This does not mean that world events or figures can't have any prophetic significance. But we must never overstate the case or use these events as authoritative guidance identifying prophecy or the return of Jesus.

Natural Disasters and Signs in the Sky

In 2017, I was interviewed for a documentary that aired on DirecTV. This documentary analyzed the popular claim that a September 23 planetary alignment would mirror the words of Revelation 12:1-4, triggering the rapture and catapulting us into the tribulation period. During my interview, I explained that Revelation 12 refers to Israel and Christ and not an apocalyptic alignment of constellations in the night sky. Others today postulate that exploding stars, meteors, and mysterious planets crashing into the earth will soon signal the inauguration of the end of time. And without fail, whenever a hurricane, earthquake, tornado, or some other natural or man-made disaster occurs, out of the woodwork come the doomsday prophets, attributing these catastrophic events to the wrath of God and a direct sign that the end is near.

Of course, if we were to see the exact environmental catastrophes and judgments on humanity as portrayed in Revelation, then we might safely conclude they were indeed prophetic fulfillments. Unfortunately, that would also mean we would already be in the seven-year tribulation period! However, this is obviously not the case, and the natural disasters we have seen cannot conclusively be assigned to God's righteous wrath. Scripture does say that in the last days "nation will rise against nation, and kingdom against kingdom, and in various places there will be famines and earthquakes" (Matthew 24:7). But there is no chapter and verse that links specific contemporary disasters to fulfilled Bible prophecy. Those judgments won't arrive until after the revealing of antichrist.

Visions and Dreams

Today, there is no shortage of self-proclaimed prophets and prophetesses claiming to have received a "prophetic word from the Lord" through some sort of supernatural vision or visitation by God in a dream. Not unlike many recent supposed trips to heaven, these "words" are given primarily to those whose theology allows for God's authoritative truth to be revealed outside of Scripture. Of the many problems with such mystical claims is that they are extremely subjective and unverifiable, resting solely on the individual's experiential claim. If I claimed that I fell and hit my head and went to heaven while unconscious, how could you refute my assertion?

Second, many of these "prophecies" are so vague (i.e., "there will be a great revival") that there's no way to know whether they ever come to pass. They are more akin to reading a horoscope or a fortune cookie, more a self-fulfilling prophecy than a divine one. We already saw in the previous two chapters that a sign of spiritual maturity is biblical discernment, and that we must test the spirits and hold those who claim to speak for God to a very high standard. A vision or dream about the end times is unnecessary because the Holy Spirit has already given divine revelation concerning these days and what is going to take place in them. God has previously and sufficiently spoken in His Word, and according to Revelation, we dare not add to it, lest we be judged (Revelation 22:18-19).

Everything Is Symbolic

To be sure, there are many symbols in Revelation's prophecies that point to literal realities. They are shadows representing substance. But to see everything through the lens of symbolism is to wildly miss the point. This final bogus method of interpreting prophecy and the end times claims that virtually all of Revelation is *symbolic*. In other words, there are no literal seal, bowl, and trumpet judgments, no actual antichrist or 144,000 Jewish male evangelists, and no real thousand-year reign of Jesus Christ upon the earth. All of these, they assert, simply refer to "spiritual principles and Christian truths."

We will examine this idea further in chapter 7. But if Revelation is nothing more than a book of symbols pointing not to realities but to ethereal truths, then who's to say what they really mean? Again, if every one of the prophecies concerning Jesus's first coming was fulfilled literally, then why wouldn't we assume prophecies related to His second coming and reign upon the earth will also be fulfilled literally? The symbolic method is vague and leaves itself open to myriad contradicting interpretations.

These errant methods of interpreting the end times illustrate how critical it is that we have a reliable process through which to understand prophecy. Each method leads you to a certain interpretive destination and understanding of Bible prophecy. Get it wrong, and you mistime the prophecies, misrepresent them, mislead others with them, or miss them altogether. Therefore, we must ensure that our approach is grounded in a solid, trustworthy method. We must apply the same principles to every prophetic passage. We do not read three-fourths of the Bible one way and then suddenly change our method of interpretation when encountering prophecy. No special deciphering goggles are needed. Just sound principles of interpretation.

Ways Through the Maze

So, what are some time-tested guidelines that will lead us into a confident understanding of the Bible's prophetic passages? Here are four fundamentals that will never let you down.

1. Interpret Literally

Ask, "What is the normal, plain understanding of the passage?" After all, the Bible wasn't written in hieroglyphics but in the plain language of the day. So ask yourself, what is the normal, grammatical, and historical understanding of the language used in the passage? This approach does not ignore symbols or figures of speech but interprets them as they were meant to be understood.

For example, Jesus said in John 10:9, "I am the door." It's easy to understand the simple and plain meaning of Jesus's use of metaphor here. Interpreting that verse *literally* does not mean we assume Jesus was claiming to be a seven-foot piece of wood that swings on a hinge. (More about symbols and figures of speech in a moment.) The point is that God intended His Word to generally be taken at face value. He meant what He said and that's why He chose the words He did. God is always intentional, and this applies to how He inspired Scripture.

We should also ask, "What did this passage mean to the original hearers or readers?" This approach assumes the authors of Scripture (whom we believe were supernaturally inspired by the Holy Spirit) recorded without error His written revelation to humankind in the original manuscripts. Therefore, when communicating this original truth, the authors would've used the most appropriate grammatical construction relevant to their ancient audience. They also would've been historically accurate and used the context of the times, such as contemporary customs and cultural practices, to help convey meaning. So, when reading any Bible passage, we take the plain, literal meaning to be the most reliable unless there is compelling reason to do otherwise (e.g., symbols, metaphors, parables).

Since God inspired every word of the Bible, meaning is found in grammatical construction and immediate context. Context is critical because the same word can have a different meaning depending on how it is used in the immediate environment of a sentence or section of Scripture. We do the same with language today. If a graduate student says, "That final exam *killed* me," we understand the meaning of the word picture as it is used in its context. Scripture has many examples of the same word having various meanings depending on the context. The Greek word for "desire" can be translated to mean immoral lust (Matthew 5:28) or godly longing (Romans 1:11), all dependent upon how it is used in the context of the passage. The word "save" has multiple meanings in the New Testament—spiritual salvation (Matthew 1:21; John 3:17), physical healing (Mark 5:23,34; Luke 7:50), deliverance from death (John 12:27), and deliverance from demons (Matthew 9:22).

When attempting to understand the Bible, context is king. So never ignore the grammatical, historical, or contextual environment of a passage of Scripture. Who wrote it? When was it written? To whom was it written? Why was it written? What does it say? How is it said?

This same approach applies to eschatological passages as well. The prophecies about Christ's first coming were literally fulfilled. They were not symbols, figures of speech, or "spiritual truths," but prophecies pointing to tangible future realities. No Bible-believing person would disagree with a literal interpretation of the prophecies related to Jesus Christ's first coming. More about these in chapter 8.

2. Don't Ignore Symbols

I've already stated that symbolic interpretation is not a reliable method, especially when arbitrarily assigning meaning to those symbols. But there are symbols in the Bible. What often derails many in the interpretation of Bible prophecy is the numerous uses of these symbols—stars, horns, bowls, beasts, heads, serpents, horse riders, and measurements of time. Because the Bible utilizes those symbols, this does not necessitate a sudden shift in the interpretive method used to understand their meaning.

A symbol is something that represents something other than itself. So the key is to find out what the symbol represents. Do this and you discover the meaning of the symbol! For example, the bowls of incense in Revelation 5:8 are symbolic of the prayers of the saints who are in heaven. We know this because it is revealed to us in the very same verse. Sometimes the meaning of a symbol is immediately explained, as in the example above, or as Mark Hitchcock notes,

> Another built-in interpretation is found in Daniel 2. Nebuchadnezzar had a dream of a metallic man with a head of gold, chest and arms of silver, belly and thighs of brass, legs of iron, and feet of iron and clay mixed. God gives Daniel the meaning of the image beginning with "the head of gold" (Daniel 2:38). The metals represent Gentile kingdoms, and the first one is Babylon. Daniel then tells the king that the other metals represent the Gentile kingdoms that will follow Babylon in succession.[2]

Revelation contains numerous examples where a symbol is explained in the immediate context or at some later point in the book. For example,

- We know that "the great city which mystically is called Sodom and Egypt" in Revelation 11:8 is actually Jerusalem.
- The woman and child of Revelation 12:1-2 are revealed as Israel and Christ.
- The phrase "a time and times and half a time" in Revelation 12:14 is previously explained in 12:6 as 1,260 days.
- The great prostitute of Revelation 17:1 is the great city, Babylon (17:18).[3]

- The ten horns of Revelation 17:12 are revealed as ten kings in the same verse.

- The seven kings (heads) of Revelation 17:9-12 are easily explained when we look at history from John's perspective in the first century.[4]

Prophetic symbols are not undecipherable and are often already explained for us in the immediate or near context. Responsible interpretation doesn't give us a license to make up our own meanings to the symbols.

3. Let Scripture Interpret Scripture

The Bible is often its own interpreter (as we saw with the previously cited symbols). But this principle applies not only in the immediate context, but also throughout the entire Bible. Scripture, including prophecy, can at times seem a bit like a puzzle, but not one that cannot be put together or understood. For example, if you read James's words in James 2:14-17 concerning the role of works in salvation, you might walk away with the idea that works are somehow a prerequisite to being saved. But Paul's writings elsewhere guard us against reaching that conclusion. When we read James and Paul together (Ephesians 2:8-9; Romans 3:28; 5:1; and Galatians 5:1-12), we can compare Scripture with Scripture and see the big picture of the puzzle. Because we believe the whole Bible is inspired by the same Holy Spirit author, it cannot, and does not, ever contradict itself (2 Peter 1:20-21).

As it relates to eschatological themes, the Bible does the same thing for us, enabling us to piece together the truth in a way that helps us better understand it. For example, the second coming of Jesus is described in its various aspects in both the Old and New Testaments (see Daniel 7:13; Zechariah 14:4; Matthew 25:31; Revelation 19:11-16). We can draw a composite portrait of the antichrist from Daniel 7:8,24-26; 9:27; 11:36-39; 2 Thessalonians 2:8-12; 1 John 2:18; and Revelation 13:1-10. Instead of random truths thrown together like a

Picasso portrait, we see instead the notes, rhythms, and harmonies contributing to a prophetic symphony.

As you seek to understand a prophetic passage (or any portion of Scripture), always ask, "Does the rest of the Bible say anything about this?"

4. Consider Prophetic Mountain Peaks and Valleys

God did not reveal all of prophecy to any one of His prophets. Some were shown only parts of the story but were denied access to other portions of the future narrative. For example, Isaiah and Micah foretold the birth of the Messiah (Isaiah 7:14; Micah 5:2). Isaiah also prophesied about the Messiah's suffering (Isaiah 53:1-12). Daniel saw the activities of the antichrist (Daniel 7:19-27). Daniel, Isaiah, Micah, and Haggai were all given glimpses of the future Messiah's kingdom (Daniel 7:13-14; Isaiah 2:1-3; Micah 4:1-2; Haggai 2:5-9). All of these are considered major "mountain peaks" in Bible prophecy.

However, none of those prophets were allowed to see the "valley" of the church, which Paul describes as being a "mystery which has been kept secret for long ages past, but now is manifest" (Romans 16:25-26; Ephesians 3:3-6).

Many years ago, while a youth pastor, my wife and I took 13 teenage girls on a two-week choir tour throughout the southeast United States (don't ask me why). It was 12 days full of fun, ministry, long hours on the road, and a fair share of teenage drama thrown in. However, one night in Florida sticks out in my mind. My wife and I stayed at the home of an elderly couple. Following dinner, we retired to the den to talk for a while. I remember being so exhausted from the long day's journey that my eyes were crossing. So, I decided to jumpstart the conversation in hopes of keeping myself awake. Reasoning from their ages that both the man and his wife must have been in their twenties or thirties during World War II, I asked, "So what did you two do during the war?"

There was a pause, and the couple glanced at one another with a look that seemed to say, "Should we tell him?" Then, almost in unison, they answered, "We worked on the Manhattan Project."

"Really?" I said, shifting myself to sit upright on the couch. "Please tell me more!"

As it turns out, the husband had been a scientist working on a portion of the Herculean secret project. That in itself was interesting, but not half as interesting as his wife's job. She revealed that she was the personal secretary to J. Robert Oppenheimer, the famed director of the Los Alamos Laboratory and head of research and design of America's first atomic bomb. That tidbit of information catapulted me into a few hours of fascinating stories.

All told, nearly half a million scientists, physicists, engineers, technicians, and other workers labored in this top-secret mission in sites scattered across the country. Because there were so many working parts in such a huge undertaking, secrecy was paramount. Therefore, the vast majority of all those Manhattan Project workers had no idea they were helping to create the world's first nuclear weapon, not until radio reports later heralded the dropping of the first bomb on Hiroshima.

Similarly, Old Testament prophets contributed to Scripture's "mountain peak" prophetic truths without knowing the full details of how their prophecies would one day come together to tell Messiah's story. For some, there was also chronological distance between one another and their original prophecies. Today, we now have the luxury of seeing the whole mountain range, and not just a peak or two.

- Some Old Testament prophecies were fulfilled within a relatively short time from their original proclamation. Other prophecies were written as if they had already been fulfilled (e.g., Isaiah 53—the Messiah's suffering, written 700 years before Christ's coming).

- Other prophecies have both a near fulfillment and a distant fulfillment. Some refer to this as a "dual or double fulfillment." My former professor at Dallas Theological Seminary, Dwight Pentecost explains:

> Two events, widely separated as to the time of their fulfillment, may be brought together into the scope of one prophecy. This was done because the prophet had a message for his own day as well as for a future time...It was the purpose of God to give the near and far view so that the fulfillment of the one should be the assurance of the fulfillment of the other.[5]

For example,

1. Moses is seen as a type of Christ (Numbers 21:9; John 3:14-15).

2. The very first prophecy in Scripture says the seed of the woman will crush the head of the serpent, a prediction outlining both the ongoing struggle between Satan and humankind as well as the promise of victory through the coming Messiah (Genesis 3:15; John 12:31; Romans 16:20; Hebrews 2:14-16; Revelation 20).[6]

3. The "abomination of desolation" in Daniel 11:31 is partially fulfilled in the acts of Antiochus Epiphanes.[7] However, Jesus said this same abomination of desolation is also a future event (Matthew 24:15-16).

4. In Luke 1:30-33, the angel Gabriel predicts both the birth of Christ and also His future reign. Four of his prophecies were realized during Jesus's earthly ministry, and three are yet to be fulfilled.

5. Joel's prophecies regarding visions, dreams, and signs in the sky (Joel 2:28-32) see part of their fulfillment at Pentecost and the birth of the church (Acts 2:17-21), while

other parts are to be fulfilled during the tribulation period (Revelation 6:12).

According to the apostle Peter, many of the Old Testament prophets carefully sought to know how and when their own prophecies would be fulfilled, and yet were prevented from knowing this (1 Peter 1:10-12). You and I have understanding they didn't have concerning even their own predictions.

In summary, the plain, literal method is the gold standard for interpreting prophetic passages, as well as the rest of the Bible. It is our primary guiding principle. All past prophecies concerning Jesus and His first coming were fulfilled literally, therefore it follows that we should expect future prophecies concerning Him to also be literally fulfilled.

When looking at prophetic passages, we should ask: Has this prophecy been fulfilled already? If so, how? And when? And if not, what future time does it point toward? What does the rest of the Bible say? Is this prophecy repeated elsewhere? Is there a near and far fulfillment of the same prophecy in Scripture? And how does this prophecy relate to Jesus (Revelation 19:10)?

When interpreting prophecy, it is important that we remain consistent in our method and approach. Jumping from one method to another will only lead to an inconsistent understanding of eschatology, resulting in more confusion. Our God is the quintessential storyteller, and prophecy is meant to both confront and to comfort, but not to confuse. A consistent hermeneutic is like an artist with a steady hand who is brush-stroking a detailed portrait. The canvas is world history, the paintbrush is the sovereign hand of God, and the oils are the hundreds of Bible prophecies used by the Almighty throughout the ages to bring to reality "the things which shall take place" (Revelation 1:19). And as we will see more fully in chapter 7, your method of interpretation will also lead you into a particular view concerning the end times.

Clairvoyants, soothsayers, shamans, and prophetic prognosticators cannot discern the times on Scripture's predictions concerning the end of days. They cannot decipher the Book nor can they accept the truth it proclaims concerning what lies ahead. They are like magicians, con artists, and sorcerers. Like the Chaldeans that once stood before Nebuchadnezzar, they are impotent and unable to interpret the meanings behind God-given revelations. Even Satan, though well versed in Scripture, is still not privy to heaven's calendar and divine timetable. And yet our God is a revealer of mysteries (Daniel 2:28).

We must remember that God's Word was written to be understood and that includes prophecy. This does not mean we know and comprehend every detail concerning the last days, Revelation, and the tribulation. It also doesn't mean there cannot be divergent views within the body of Christ. But as we saw earlier in this book, the meaning of prophecy often becomes clearer the closer we get to its fulfillment.

Without a literal, historical, grammatical, and contextual interpretation of Bible prophecy, none of Scripture's end-times prophecies make much sense. However, with this method, you can use your Bible to unlock prophecy's secrets and understand the times as God's plan unfolds.

First-century believers were marked by an overwhelming anticipation for the return of Jesus Christ for His bride. How much greater should our expectation be today, now that it appears God's last-days prophecies are finally coming into focus?

Are you ready?

Chapter 6

Exploring Scripture's Unfulfilled Prophecies

Christian Hype or Coming Reality?

Heaven and earth will pass away, but
My words will not pass away.

MATTHEW 24:35

God still has some unfinished business regarding Bible prophecy. When the first century came to a close, Scripture's prophetic story appears to have been suddenly interrupted. Jesus's earthly ministry, His death and resurrection, and the mysterious and miraculous phenomenon of the church, were all prophesied beforehand and saw their fulfillment. But with the last stroke of Revelation's pen around AD 95, Bible prophecy was paused, set aside for renewal at a predetermined, future date. And for 2,000 years, we have been waiting expectantly for the next event that would signal the restarting of heaven's prophetic broadcast, a time indicating the end-times countdown has officially begun.

So the question for informed Christians is not whether these future prophecies are going to take place, but *when* and *how* they will occur.

What Lies Ahead

With all the prophecies previously fulfilled through the first coming of Christ and the birth of the church, should we expect any more to become reality? Are there any pending prophecies? What's in store for the church and the rest of humanity? What future history has God already documented in His Word? Will God set Revelation's events in motion?

Using the literal interpretive method we discussed in the previous chapter, hundreds of Scripture's prophecies are yet to be fulfilled. Of those, here are 15 that are major "mountain peaks" in view on the not-too-distant horizon.

1. The Rapture (John 14:3; 1 Corinthians 15:51-58; 1 Thessalonians 4:13-18; Revelation 3:10)

Scripture indicates the next event on God's prophetic calendar is this glorious event early Christians called "the blessed hope" (Titus 2:13). Prior to the release of God's unimaginable wrath on a rebellious planet, Jesus will return in the air to rescue His bride, snatching her away to the Father's house, the place He has been preparing for us these past 2000 years (John 14:1-3). Although the word *rapture* is not found in Scripture's original Greek text, the teaching of the rapture is. In fact, two Greek words describe this event. One is *parousia*, meaning "presence or arrival." It is typically translated as the "*coming* of the Lord."[1] The other word Paul uses to picture the rapture is *harpazo*, a unique verb meaning to "seize, capture, carry off by force, claim for oneself or suddenly snatch away."[2] We will look more at the timing of the rapture in the next chapter, but it is my view that this event will take place prior to the tribulation period. In other words, it hasn't happened yet.

2. The Bema (Romans 14:10; 1 Corinthians 3:9-15; 4:1-5; 9:24-27; 2 Corinthians 5:10)

The Bible tells us that following the rapture of the church there will be a ceremony in heaven known as the *bema*, or the judgment seat of

Christ. In ancient athletic games, the bema was a raised platform upon which the judge of the games sat. There, victorious athletes would receive their rewards and crowns. The purpose of believers individually appearing before Christ is made clear to us. This judgment has to do with rewards, not sins or sin. At this future event, the Lord Himself will review every Christian's life, and His praise and rewards will be given according to what we did for Him while on the earth. Our motives will also be evaluated. This prophecy is a gamechanger because it tells us that what we do for the kingdom and cause of the Lord Jesus Christ really does matter (1 Corinthians 15:58).

3. The Marriage of the Lamb (John 3:27-29; 2 Corinthians 11:2; Revelation 19:6-8)

Genuine believers (the church) are portrayed in Scripture as the bride of Christ (Ephesians 5:25-27). Having chosen us before the foundation of the world (Ephesians 1:3-4), the Father betrothed us to his Son in real time at the moment of salvation. The Holy Spirit was given to us as a "pledge" (down payment) of God's commitment to consummate our salvation in Christ (Ephesians 1:13-14). The rapture pictures the ancient Jewish custom of snatching away the bride (Matthew 25:1-13), after which the wedding would be consummated and the wedding feast would begin. Following Jesus's rescue of the church, our union with Him will complete our salvation, and "so we shall always be with the Lord" (1 Thessalonians 4:17). This is not the same as the marriage supper of the Lamb, which will take place during the millennial kingdom on the earth and will involve both Old Testament saints and those believers from the tribulation (Matthew 22:1-14; 25:1-13; Luke 12:37; 14:16-24; Revelation 19:9).

4. Seven Years of Tribulation and God's Wrath on Earth (Revelation 6–19)

When John penned the supernatural vision given him by Jesus around AD 95, he could not possibly have fully understood the implications of such an apocalypse. Though some may retroactively see some of Revelation's prophecies as having been fulfilled in the first century (Nero = antichrist, AD 70 fall of Jerusalem = abomination of desolation), Scripture and world history point to the contrary. First, Revelation is a record of future prophetic occurrences, not a historical record of past events. If John is merely recounting what has already happened, then the book loses most of its prophetic significance. Second, internal and external evidence points to Revelation being written at the close of the first century, not in the mid-sixties as some have believed.[3] This effectively discounts what is known as the preterist view. Third, the global catastrophes and judgments so graphically described in chapters 6–19 simply have not occurred in the past 2,000 years.

Revelation documents future worldwide famine; one-fourth of the world's population dying by disease; full-scale wars; meteors; giant hailstones; fire; sea life destroyed; skies blackened; demonic creatures terrorizing humanity; four foul demons killing another one-third of mankind; godlessness; murder; immorality; sorcery and demon worship; massive theft and looting; a plague of boils; seas, rivers, and springs turning to blood; intense solar heat; a plague of darkness; the most powerful earthquake in human history; global panic; death and devastation; a Satan-possessed world leader who requires you to worship him; and much, much more. The question is, "Have all these, at any point since they were written, ever appeared and in a seven-year time span?" The answer is no. These horrific judgments are yet future and await those who refuse Jesus's offer of salvation.

Therefore, we're still looking at a *future* fulfillment of those prophecies.

5. The Battle of Gog and Magog (Ezekiel 38–39)

During the tribulation's unprecedented seven years of mass misery, the nation of Israel will rise to the forefront of international news. The first major occurrence will be a groundbreaking peace treaty in the Middle East, brokered by the man of sin—the antichrist (Daniel 9:27). The signing of this treaty officially marks the beginning of the tribulation period.[4] Six hundred years before the birth of Christ, the prophet Ezekiel wrote that in the "latter years" Israel will be "gathered from many nations to the mountains of Israel" (Ezekiel 38:8). In that day, the Jewish nation will finally experience a sense of peace after decades of war and terrorist attacks. She also will be dwelling securely in the land. However, during this time an alliance of surrounding nations, led by Gog (their leader) will invade the tiny Jewish nation. Their goal? To eradicate the Hebrews from history and erase Israel off the map.

Interestingly, this attack also challenges antichrist's authority as well, as he is responsible for the peace that has for so long evaded this region of the world. This ten-nation force is comprised of Magog (Central Asian nations of the former Soviet Union), Rosh (Russia), Meshech and Tubal (modern-day Turkey), Persia (Iran), Ethiopia/Cush (Sudan), Put (Libya), Gomer (Turkey), and Beth-togarmah (Turkey). With the exception of Russia, these nations today are exclusively Muslim. Because she is at peace and dwelling securely in the land, Israel will be caught off guard by this massive invasion. But before the antichrist and his ten-nation alliance have an opportunity to defend the peace he brokered, Another steps in with divine intervention.

It is a classic David versus Goliath matchup. And as He did in centuries past, the God of Israel shows up to fight for Israel and win the day. The Almighty executes a four-fold, supernatural military strategy:

First, a significant earthquake occurs in Israel, severely disrupting and crippling the invading armies (Ezekiel 38:18-20). God says He sends this earthquake because of His "fury," "anger," "zeal," and "blazing wrath" (vv. 18-19). This tells us that even during the tribulation, God's unconditional covenant with Abraham and his seed is still in effect, as He swore to "bless those who bless you, and the one who curses you I will curse" (Genesis 12:3).

Second, God causes the enemy armies to turn on each other,

perhaps a confusing effect brought on by the great earthquake (Ezekiel 38:21).

Third, He sends a sudden disease among the troops as a part of His judgment on them (v. 22).

And finally, from the sky comes "a torrential rain, with hailstones, fire and brimstone" (v. 22).

The scripturally stated endgame of God's vindication of Israel is that He would magnify Himself and make Himself known among many nations (v. 23). In judgment, as in salvation, God declares Himself to be the sovereign Lord of the universe.

Mark Hitchcock writes, "These nations will brashly swoop down on Israel to take her land, but the only piece of land they will claim in Israel will be their own burial plots (Ezekiel 39:12). They will set out to bury Israel. But God will bury them."[5]

So how do we know this prophecy is still future and not already fulfilled as some have claimed? To begin with, in order for this prophecy to be fulfilled, the Jewish people must be regathered from many nations back to the land of Israel. This began in earnest in 1948 when Israel officially became a nation again. Since that time, Jews from all over the world have made their way back to the land of their forefathers. Today, more Jews are living in Israel than at any time in 20 centuries.

Second, for this prophecy to occur, the Jews must also be "living securely" in the land and in the "last days" (Ezekiel 38:8,11,14,16). This is currently not a reality, as Israel remains on constant alert from the Gaza Strip, with some 11,000 rockets having been launched against the Jews since 2005 and 630 launched in 2011 alone.[6] By anyone's estimation, Israel is far from *living securely* in the land. I do not see this secure status becoming a reality until the antichrist's peace treaty goes into effect at the beginning of the tribulation.

Third, this Ezekiel 38–39 war must take place between the time Israel is gathered back to the homeland (Ezekiel 37) and the time of her spiritual rebirth as recorded in Ezekiel 40–48. I believe this rebirth will happen at the inauguration of the millennial kingdom.

Lastly, there is no historical record, biblically or from secular sources, of any such invasion ever occurring in the Old Testament or intertestamental period.[7] Therefore, we must consider this Battle of Gog and Magog as future, and thus unfulfilled, prophecy.

6. Jesus's Second Coming (Revelation 19:11-16; Isaiah 24:1-6; 63:1-5)

The climactic crescendo of Revelation comes in chapter 19 with the prophesied arrival of the glorified Christ. No longer portrayed in Scripture as the humble carpenter-rabbi from Nazareth, this Jesus is risen, exalted, crowned King of kings, and coming back with a brutal wrath agenda in His heart (2 Thessalonians 1:6-8). He is described as having a golden crown on His head and a sharp sickle in His hand (Revelation 14:14). The Christ whom John sees in Revelation 1 also has eyes that are a flame of fire in chapter 19 (v. 12). A sharp sword of slaughter proceeds from his mouth (v. 15). He is called "Faithful and True" and "King of kings, and Lord of lords" (17:14; 19:11,16). But He also has a cryptic name written on Him which no one knows but Himself (19:12). His return catches them all by surprise, like a thief in the night (Matthew 24:27,30,43-44; 1 Thessalonians 5:2-5; 2 Peter 3:10; Revelation 16:15; 19:11-21).

In this prophecy, the armies of the earth assemble at the close of the many-faceted battle campaign of Armageddon (Revelation 16:12-16; 19:19-21; 2 Thessalonians 2:8; Psalm 2:9; Isaiah 34:1-7; 63:1-6; Joel 3:9-21; Zechariah 12:1-9; 14:1-5). Unexpectedly breaking through the clouds, Jesus touches down on the very place from which He had ascended centuries previous—the Mount of Olives (Acts 1:11-12). The impact of His feet touching the ground triggers a massive earthquake, splitting the famed mountain in half (Zechariah 14:4). He will then, in what has been called the "Battle of Jerusalem," destroy the armies gathered outside the holy city in the valley of Jehoshaphat (Joel 3:9-17).[8] Jesus then turns His attention east, into what today is Jordan, to rescue the Jewish remnant who have been hiding there since the abomination of desolation three-and-a-half years earlier (Revelation 12:6-14; Isaiah 34:1-7; 63:1-5; Joel 3:19).

Lastly, this conquering King heads west for a rendezvous with a rebellious humanity. Riding upon His galloping white steed of victory toward the Plain of Esdraelon (Har-Magedon), He encounters Earth's military forces marshalled there. Having been lured and summoned to this location by three demonic spirits, they are locked and loaded in preparation "for the war of the great day of God, the Almighty" (Revelation 16:13-16). Perhaps originally assembled to try once again to wipe Israel from the earth, their attention and military strategy are quickly diverted toward the Rider in the sky wearing the blood-stained robe (Isaiah 34:6; 63:1-6). Behold, the deception of satanic forces married with the inherent wicked, proud human heart (Genesis 3:1-5; Jeremiah 17:9; Romans 3:10-12; Ephesians 2:1-3; 6:12; 1 Peter 5:8). Even at the close of history, humankind will fall prey to believing they can become like God and to even defeat Him in battle.

What happens next can only be described as incomprehensible horror and brutal slaughter.

An angel issues a worldwide invitation to all the birds of the earth to come feast on the corpses of kings, commanders, the mighty, and the common, along with their horses (Revelation 19:17-18). The beast (antichrist) and the false prophet from Revelation 13 are seized and baptized into the newly revealed lake of fire, which burns with brimstone (19:20). This Jesus merely utters a word of judgment, and millions gathered on that vast battlefield instantly meet their death. It's the vengeance of the Almighty upon His unrepentant, rebellious enemies. In a moment, they collectively breathe their last, crossing the threshold from this life to the next. And all the birds fill their bellies with their unrighteous flesh (19:15,21). This future bloodshed and devastation is unparalleled in human history. The "great and terrible day of the LORD" has come, and they are defenseless against Him (Joel 2:31; Malachi 4:5; Revelation 16:14).

No one can truly comprehend the carnage and aftermath of such a scene. But as gory as it certainly will be, the Bible tells us it is a judgment and battle waged in righteousness. If ever there was a just war, it is the one that ends at Armageddon.

7. Israel's Judgment (Ezekiel 20:30-39; Matthew 25:1-30)

When God uses numbers to refer to events, we can always be assured of their accuracy. The 1260 days prophesied for both halves of the tribulation are meant to be taken literally (Revelation 11:1-3; 12:6; 13:5). However, when this seven-year season comes to a close, there is a parenthesis of time between Jesus's return and the inauguration of His millennial reign. According to the prophet Daniel, there is an interval of 75 days, essentially a month and a half, divided into 30-day and 45-day periods (Daniel 12:11-12). Some have suggested that the 30 days prophesied in Daniel allows for time to restore a ravaged landscape in preparation for life in the coming millennial kingdom. And this is certainly possible. But it also appears to be the time when Israel will be judged. God had promised to Israel a continuation of the Davidic kingdom over which the future Messiah would reign (2 Samuel 7; 1 Chronicles 17:1-15; 2 Chronicles 6:16-17; Isaiah 9:6-7; 11:1-5; Jeremiah 23:5-6; 30:9; Luke 1:32-33,68-71; Acts 13:32-37; Revelation 3:7). It follows that those Jews surviving the tribulation (the remnant) would be the first to pass under His judgment and allowed to enter into the kingdom. Those Jews who believed the message concerning the Messiah proclaimed to them during the tribulation are the "wise virgins" of Matthew 25:1-7.[9] These will enter into the joy of their Master in the millennial kingdom (Matthew 25:21).[10]

Tracking with the chronology of Jesus's teaching in Matthew 24–25, the prophetic timeline lays out as follows: tribulation period (24:4-26), second coming (24:27-31), judgment of Israel (25:1-30), and judgment of Gentiles (25:31-46).

8. Gentile Judgment (Matthew 25:31-46)

Jesus will judge all those Gentiles who endured the tribulation and came out alive on the other end. All those who worshipped the beast by taking his mark (the "goats") will be separated from God and sent "into the eternal fire which has been prepared for the devil and his angels" (Matthew 25:41). The righteous living ("sheep") who are destined to inherit the kingdom will likely join the rest of the redeemed and begin the celebration of the marriage supper of the Lamb in the millennium (Revelation 19:7-10).

9. Satan's Binding (Revelation 20:1-3)

During the American Revolutionary War, colonial military intelligence devised an ingenious plan. They constructed a massive, 500-yard-long iron chain that spanned the width of the Hudson River in upstate New York. The idea was that any British ships attempting to navigate the slow S-curve in the river at that point would be caught by the huge chain and destroyed. The exact location of that chain blockade later became the United States Military Academy at West Point. On display there today is a portion of the chain. While my son was at West Point, I visited him there many times and was able to see and hold those heavy links, which became known as the Great Chain.

Revelation tells us of another "great chain." This one is used, not to block ships, but to bind eternity's most dangerous criminal. Following the bloodbath of Armageddon, John sees an angel descending from heaven with a "great chain" in his hand (Revelation 20:1). But also in his hand is a unique key, which matches the lock on what is called the "abyss." This dreaded abyss is well known to Satan and the demonic host he commands.[11] There are seven mentions of this bottomless abyss in Revelation, and each time it refers to a place where demons are tormented, isolated, and chained (Revelation 9:1-2; 11:7; 17:8; 20:1,3). Peter tells us this pit is characterized by darkness and also houses the perverted demons who cohabitated with mortal women in Genesis 6 (2 Peter 2:4; Jude 6; Genesis 6:1-4). This heavenly angel holding the abyss key grabs Satan, here also called "the dragon, the serpent of old, who is the devil," and binds him with the great chain (Revelation 20:1-3).

Some Christians today practice what is called "binding Satan" through prayer or by simply declaring it "in the name of Jesus" in an attempt to deny the devil access to a specific location or prevent him from influencing people. However, nowhere in Scripture is this practice taught.[12] We are never commanded to "bind Satan," and outside of this future prophetic passage, he is never said to be bound. On the contrary, even Michael the archangel refused to rebuke the devil in his angelic authority when confronting him about the body of Moses. Instead, he called upon the Lord to do so (Jude 6). By contrast, we are told we can "resist" this unbound devil, and also that we can "flee" from him (James 4:7; 1 Peter 5:9). Further, by outfitting ourselves with the armor of God, we can also "stand firm against the schemes of the devil" (Ephesians 6:11). If we had the power to simply bind Satan whenever we wanted, then why would God tell us to resist him, flee from him, and stand firm against him? Revelation 20:1-3 is the only instance in Scripture where the devil is bound, and even then it's done by a special angel from heaven.

In a gesture signifying great power and authority, this same angel throws Satan into the bottomless pit (abyss). He then shuts the door and seals it over him. And there the devil will remain for 1,000 years. No longer to deceive the nations, the prince of darkness is kept in his own darkness of solitary confinement.

10. The Saints' Resurrection (Daniel 12:1-3; Isaiah 26:19; Revelation 20:4)

There are two resurrections mentioned in Revelation 20—one a resurrection to eternal life and the other to eternal damnation. From a comparison of Scripture, it appears that Old Testament saints (not a part of the church raised from the grave at the rapture) and those who were martyred or died during the tribulation are the ones brought to life in this first resurrection. These tribulation saints perished at the hands of the beast and his forces (Revelation 6:9-11; 20:4), having their heads hacked off with an axe or sawed off with a knife, perhaps similar to what is practiced today by the barbaric death cult of radical Islam.

11. Jesus's Thousand-Year Reign (Revelation 20:4-6)

Scripture devotes a great deal of attention to the millennial kingdom of Christ (Isaiah 2:1-5; 11:1-16; 32:1-20; 35:1-10; 60:1-22; Jeremiah 31:1-40; 33:1-26; Ezekiel 37:14-28; Amos 9:11-15; Zechariah 14:6-21). The Gospels tell us of a future kingdom prophesied by both John the Baptist and Jesus (Matthew 3:2; 8:11; Mark 1:14-15). It is during this kingdom, according to Acts 3:21, when "all things" will be restored. Also in this kingdom, Jesus will be physically present on the earth, ruling from David's throne (Isaiah 11:1-2; 55:3; Jeremiah 23:5-8; 33:20-26; Ezekiel 34:23-24; 37:24-28; Hosea 3:5; Micah 4:6-8). Promises God made to Abraham concerning the patriarch's seed, the land, and Israel's possession of it are also fulfilled during this time (Isaiah 10:20-27; 19:24-25; 43:1; 65:8-9; Jeremiah 30:18-22; 32:36-39; Ezekiel 34:23-24,30-31; Micah 7:19-20; Zechariah 13:9; Malachi 3:16-18). In this 1,000-year earthly reign, Jesus will assume His regal role as the Messiah-King. His kingdom will be marked by righteousness, a stunning contrast to the world in which you and I currently live, and even more so compared to the world of tribulation. Only the righteous ones are admitted to this kingdom (Matthew 25:34-40).

Another aspect of Jesus's millennial reign will be peace, as finally the Prince of Peace presides over paradise (Isaiah 9:6). There He rewards the faithful by giving them rule and authority in the kingdom (Daniel 7:18,21-22,27; 1 Corinthians 6:1-3; Revelation 2:26-28; 20:4-6). Believers will share some governing role over the nations. Like shepherds, they will care for the rest, following Christ's lead. And in some capacity, Christians will even govern godly angels. What we do now and how we use what has been given to us will determine the nature and extent of our reward and reign in that day (1 Corinthians 3:10-15; 2 Corinthians 5:10-11).

Sin's curse on creation will be reversed as well. Romans 8:22 tells us that presently the "whole creation groans and suffers" from Adam's sin. We live in a fallen world where animals and plants are impacted by sin's curse. But in this coming kingdom, for which we have all prayed in the Lord's Prayer, creation will be set right again. His kingdom will have come, His will on earth will finally be done as it is in heaven (Matthew 6:10). Nature will be brought back into a heavenly harmony, where the wolf and the lamb will lie down together. Deserts will produce blossoming plants, and even the snakes won't bite (Isaiah 11:6-9; 35:1-7)!

And best of all, everyone will worship the Lamb, the King, Messiah, and Savior, Jesus Christ (Isaiah 45:23; 52:7-10; 66:18-23; Zephaniah 3:8-11; Zechariah 14:16; Malachi 1:11; Revelation 5:9-14).

12. Satan's Release and Final Rebellion (Revelation 20:7-10)

In what is often seen as a confusing move causing Christians to scratch their heads, God unchains the devil, allowing him the freedom to once again deceive the nations. Though we're not told, presumably the same angel who bound Satan and threw him into the bottomless pit is the one who unshackles and releases him. But why would God ever want to release the one in whom evil itself was born? What's the point? Why not just keep him there where he belongs and where he can do no more damage?

To begin unpacking this mystery, understand that many believers from the tribulation will move right into the millennial kingdom. They will still possess their earthly physical bodies and will be able to produce offspring during this 1,000-year period. In fact, so many are eventually born over this period that their number "is like the sand of the seashore" (Revelation 20:8). Called the "nations," these unredeemed people are duped by the devil. Alone in his dark cell for ten centuries, he has time to reflect. He also has time to crave the global authority and worship he briefly enjoyed during the tribulation. This worship was suddenly denied when the glorified Son of God burst through the clouds, crashing Satan's wicked worldwide party. But don't have sympathy for the devil. He is unchanged, and even more intentionally evil than ever before. Ponder that if you can.

In just a "short time" following his release, he amasses a huge rebellion made up of peoples from all over the earth, collectively known as "Gog and Magog" (Revelation 20:3,8).[13] Surrounding Jerusalem, the epicenter of Messiah's kingdom, they prepare to lay siege to the city, kill its inhabitants, and overthrow its King. Jesus's victory at Armageddon, though decisive and thorough, is now a 1,000-year memory in the misled minds of Satan's new army. This is a generation of the freshly fooled. And their sin natures partner with the Luciferian lie that says true freedom exists apart from submission to the Savior.

But this battle campaign never really gets off the ground, as God sends a furious firestorm from heaven to "devour them" (Revelation 20:9). But why even let this happen? One thing this future episode demonstrates is that even an idyllic environment, and one where righteousness is exalted and practiced, is powerless to remedy or curtail the depravity of the human heart. Only a supernatural rebirth from within can transform the sin-sick soul of every person ever born, whether now or in that day.

Second, it also illustrates that Satan never changes, and indeed he can't. He is unredeemable, and the Son would have to incarnate as an angelic being and suffer eternal torment on behalf of angels for salvation to happen. Satan is pure, undiluted evil. And he will never be anything else.

Third, it shows us that God cannot be overcome by evil, even by the lord of evil himself. There is no duality of forces in the universes. No *Star Wars* "dark side" of an otherwise good "force." God is infinitely more pure and powerful than the devil and all his angels. And the swift squelching of this rebellion proves this point.

Finally, from this final purge of sin and sinners from the universe we learn that God sometimes even uses evil to accomplish His sovereign purposes (Acts 2:22-23; 4:27-30).

The devil who decided to once again deceive the nations is himself again "thrown" somewhere, this time into the lake of fire and brimstone. There, he joins his former colleagues, the beast (antichrist) and false prophet. Their sentence? To be "tormented day and night forever and ever" (Revelation 20:10).

13. God's Great White Throne Judgment (Revelation 20:11-15)

The next prophecy depicts what is perhaps the most frightening scene in all of Scripture. Here God turns His attention toward those unrepentant souls who have been kept in hell following their deaths. They are all brought up before the Judge of humankind. His name is the Lord Jesus Christ, and the Father has given all judgment into His hands (John 5:22-23; Acts 17:30-31; 2 Timothy 4:1).

The following is a picture of God's wrath and the fate of all those who reject Jesus's offer of salvation in this life (Revelation 14:9-11). For these, there is "no rest day and night" and the "smoke of their torment goes up forever and ever." There is no pardon and no reprieve. No chance to rest, even for one minute. No second chances for salvation. For they all knew God existed. They heard His truth. And they willfully chose to remain in their sin. They are the damned of eternity.

And they chose to be there.

God, not the devil, rules over this hellish lake of fire.[14] And like incense in the temple, their sulfurous smoke rises before the One who superintends such judgment, a perpetual reminder that He is righteous, and that "all His ways are just" (Deuteronomy 32:4; Psalm 18:30; 145:17).

John sees this glorified Christ, the same intimidating Sovereign God before whom the beloved disciple had previously fallen on his face like a dead man (Revelation 1:17). Only this time Jesus is sitting on what is called a "great white throne" (20:11). And how do the unsaved respond to this throne? Understandably, they want to run and hide, to flee for safety from Him who sits on the throne. But they are unable. They have been issued a divine summons to appear before the universe's Supreme Court. As the Judge is omniscient and omnipresent, there is nowhere to hide, even in the grave or the depths of the sea (20:13). Though some may escape justice in this life, you can be certain they will not avoid it in the next.

They're all there. The great and the small, from every tribe, race, and nation. They all make an appearance before this throne. Kings and commoners. Rich and poor. Famous and obscure. Pagan and religious. The morally upright and those who conspired acts of evil. Any person who embraced or placed faith in anyone or anything besides Jesus (John 14:6; Acts 4:12). Being Jewish, Catholic, or Baptist counts for nothing before this throne. Only those who through faith alone in Christ alone by grace alone will avoid this dreadful date with Deity.

Next, books are opened that record in detail each person's deeds while on earth (Revelation 20:12-13). It is not that these deeds themselves save or condemn them, but they reveal the fruit of their lives and the root of their hearts. Jesus taught that trees are known by their fruit (Matthew 7:15-20). This becomes Exhibit A in the case against each individual. According to Scripture, there will be varying degrees of eternal punishment, proving that not all sin is the same (Romans 2:6,9,16; Matthew 11:22-24; 12:36-37).

Exhibit B is presented. Another book. This one is called the "book of life" (Revelation 20:12). This heavenly book contains the names of every person chosen before the foundation of the world, and who, in time, believed on Christ to forgive and save them (Luke 10:20). If you're certain your name is in this book, you should rejoice. If not, then you should repent.

This great white throne judgment officially marks the end of physical death and Hades, as they are both disposed of into the lake of fire (Revelation 20:14). Funerals are a thing of the past. Graves are gone. A new era has begun.

14. The Heavens and Earth Destroyed (Matthew 24:35; 2 Peter 3:3-13; Revelation 21:1)

A once-popular Christian statement, "It's all gonna burn," was a reminder to us not to become too attached to material possessions or the things of this world. As it turns out, that's exactly what Scripture says. After Jesus's millennial reign, God will dispose of the current heaven and earth: "the heavens will pass away with a roar and the elements will be destroyed with intense heat, and the earth and its works will be burned up" (2 Peter 3:10). This event is called the "day of the Lord" or the "day of God" (2 Peter 3:10,12). This phrase "the day of the Lord" is used about 21 times in the Old and New Testaments to describe coming judgments. God is going to destroy everything we know of this earth and the universe. They will no longer exist. The certainty of this prophecy, Peter says, is a sobering reality and wake-up call. He urges us to nurture godly character, exhibit holy conduct, and adopt an eager expectation of the future we have with Him. That's because, with Jesus, the best is yet to come. Yes, it's all gonna burn.

15. The New Heavens and Earth (Isaiah 65:17; 66:22; 2 Peter 3:13; Revelation 21:1,9–22:5)

Now, without the old heaven and earth, God, who originally spoke the universe into existence, creates new ones in their places. The word John uses to describe this phenomenon is *kainos* (new), signifying something fresh, not like before. It's something new in quality. The new heaven and earth will not be fixer-upper versions of the old ones. Rather, they will be as of yet unimagined new ones. Also, descending out of heaven will be a new Jerusalem, a massive cubed city where all the saints live (Hebrews 12:22-24; Revelation 21:10-27). Measuring 1,500 miles high, 1,500 miles long, and 1,500 miles wide, and with jasper walls 216 feet thick, this city hovers downward, eventually coming to rest on the earth (Hebrews 11:10). Admittedly, it's hard for our minds to comprehend such an odd-sounding dwelling place—with gold streets, gates of pearl, a crystal-clear river of water flowing from

God's throne, and the long-awaited return of the tree of life (Genesis 2:9; Revelation 22:1-2). Our spirits will have to be glorified and our bodies remade in order to understand this and withstand the magnitude and majesty of our eternal home.

Keep in mind, none of these prophecies have been fulfilled at any time throughout the past 2,000 years. Attempts to spiritualize these concrete predictions only leave us more confused, uncertain, and even skeptical. To explain away these prophecies by saying they merely represent "spiritual values" or symbolize some future aspect of our salvation is to completely miss the authorial intent of Scripture's writers. It opens Bible prophecies to being interpreted a variety of ways.

But God has plainly laid all this out for us in His Word. We complicate it and confuse ourselves when we fail to accept them as clearly written. And what is clear is that these forecast phenomena are yet to occur.

At the end of John's Revelation, he shares several things that will one day be extinct in God's unfolding prophetic future. For believers, there won't be any more tears, death, mourning, crying, or pain (21:4). The reason for this, Jesus says, is because He is "making all things *new*" (21:5). Best of all, John records, God Himself will dwell among us (21:3). That, above all things, makes heaven, *heaven*. And at long last, the deepest longing of the human heart will be fulfilled.

Right along with all these glorious prophecies.

Chapter 7

Examining the Major Views on Prophecy

Contradictions, Clarity, and Consensus

Without belief in a biblical eschatology,
there is no Christian hope.

ALBERT MOHLER

When discussing Bible prophecy, three obstacles emerge that perpetually threaten our grasp on this important subject. They are ignorance, confusion, and apathy. Let's explore each of them here.

Ignorance

Although 77 percent of evangelicals believe we are living in the end times, a much smaller percentage appear to know much about what Scripture says concerning these last days. As a result, many Christians' understanding of Revelation and end-times events resembles more a Picasso-like portrait than the story portrayed in God's Word. When forming their own understanding of prophecy, many American Christians are left to assemble random tidbits they've collected over the years. Their understanding of Bible prophecy is woefully inadequate and inept. And why wouldn't it be when the vast majority of pastors avoid teaching through Revelation or covering the subject?

In short, we just don't talk about it, and this produces a pervasive ignorance that has settled across the body of Christ like an ever-present cloud bank. Even worse, Christians are not reading the Bible itself very much at all.[1] What is also alarming is that the interaction with Scripture among millennials is drastically less than that of the previous generation.[2] This biblical illiteracy is a scathing indictment on pastors, churches, and Christians all across America.

This epidemic is made more tragic by the fact that the apostles devoted much of their written ministries helping Christians know, not guess, their way through doctrine and life.

Confusion

What information the church does have about the end times is often self-contradictory. Of course, there are many areas of doctrine over which theologians, Christians, and churches disagree. Whether it's predestination, baptism, the gifts of the Holy Spirit, or even worship and evangelism, there is no shortage of doctrinal debate in the body of Christ. And the doctrine of eschatology is certainly no exception to this. It has already been stated that we do not talk enough about Bible prophecy. And yet when we do, we tend to disagree. These varying views often break down along denominational lines, with Lutherans, Presbyterians, and Episcopalians generally at odds with Baptists, Pentecostals, and nondenominational churches. And even within those breakdowns there can be further division and diverse views. This can create confusion within the bride of Christ, a sort of doctrinal disorientation. And because we have no real consensus, we also have no unified voice with which to build up one another or warn the world.

Apathy

I once took a young student pastor to lunch in order to encourage him in his ministry. When I asked him what he was currently doing with his teenagers, he enthusiastically responded, "Well, I'm taking our middle school boys through a detailed study of the furniture of the Old Testament tabernacle." (Insert screeching brakes sound here.)

I almost choked on my salsa.

I remember thinking, *This guy needs to sell all he has, take the money, and go buy himself a clue!* Of all the things you could spend weeks discussing with teenage boys, the tabernacle furniture would not make it into my top 100 list.

I find that a lot of Christians view Bible prophecy like they do the tabernacle furniture. Unnecessary. Irrelevant. Like, what's the point? You'll be happy to know that Bible prophecy is exponentially more important and applicable to our lives than the tabernacle furniture. Most Christians don't think much about eschatology and, quite frankly, don't care, either. And for this reason we must show them *why* they should care. As with many other areas of Bible teaching, there must always be a powerful "So what?" for the listener. "How does this make a difference in my life?" Without making this relevant connection, truth taught often becomes truth lost. And forgotten. Application imprints the Word in our minds and hearts, making a lasting impression in our lives.

Many pastors and Christians I meet have never been shown the relevance of Bible prophecy to their daily lives. And isn't that where we all live? In the *daily*? We exist in the everyday struggles and responsibilities of life. We struggle enough just knowing how the *rest* of the Bible intersects with our lives. But once we venture outside of the Gospels, some of the epistles, and a few psalms and proverbs, things get a little sketchy when it comes to understanding and application. This is especially true with "all that prophecy stuff," because, after all, it hasn't even happened yet! And that's one reason why many simply don't care or see the need for studying Bible prophecy. We privately reason that if no one definitively knows how, when, or even why prophecy will occur in the future, then it must not be all that important. I mean, God always makes the important things clear to us, right? And since prophecy seems unclear, it must not be that big of a deal. Therefore, we probably shouldn't spend too much time trying to figure it out.

At least that's how many people think.

In this chapter, I hope to help erase some of the symptoms associated with these three obstacles—ignorance, confusion, and apathy. Through biblical information and clarification of the major views of eschatology, I trust you will have a better understanding of these things and how their relevance does (or does not) intersect with your life.

What's Your View?

There's a famous story of six blind men who were invited to touch an elephant and describe their impression of it. One man touched the elephant's leg and said the elephant was like a pillar. Another man touched his tail and said it was like a rope. The third man touched his trunk and described it as the branch of a tree. The fourth man put his hand on the side of the elephant and said it felt like a wall. The fifth man grabbed a tusk and described it as a large pipe. and the sixth man felt the elephant's ear and called it a fan. This fictitious story has been used to justify the belief that all religions lead to God, it's just that we all describe Him differently. But what this parable fails to communicate is that all the men were wrong. While each of them had a personal impression of what the elephant was, none of them could accurately describe the entire elephant. That's because they were all blind!

When explaining the doctrine of eschatology, we can't all be right, though there may be some points of agreement. However, there are at least two things that most everyone in Christendom agrees on—Jesus Christ is coming back, and the book of Revelation is in the Bible. That may not be much, but it's something. Beyond that, our theological roads diverge. A lot. The big question is, how and when is Jesus returning, and what does Revelation really mean? In mainstream Christianity, there are four major interpretations of Revelation's prophecies.

1. The preterist interpretation
2. The historicist interpretation
3. The futurist interpretation

4. The timeless interpretation

The Preterist View

Preterist Interpretation

This view claims Revelation was fulfilled around AD 70 with the Roman general Titus's conquest of Jerusalem. At this time the temple was destroyed and the Jews were scattered all over the world. *Preterist* means "past," and here it signifies that the events described in Revelation have already happened and therefore have no future relevance as prophecy.

There are two subviews within this interpretation, an extremely liberal one and the other a more moderate understanding. A liberal preterist would spiritualize such things as resurrections and the new heavens and the new earth. A moderate preterist would say the millennial kingdom is happening now and not in a future 1,000-year period. However, the moderate preterist would still believe in a literal second coming of Jesus, and yet still see the rest of Revelation as past "history," though largely spiritualized.

Preterism interprets Jesus's words in Matthew 24:34, "Truly I say to you, this generation will not pass away until all these things take place" as indicating His prophecies would be fulfilled sometime in the first century. This view, then, requires Revelation to have been written sometime around AD 65, obviously before the fall of Jerusalem in AD 70.

If preterism is true, and Revelation has already happened, then there is:

- No seven-year tribulation
- No coming apostasy
- No last days, as they already happened in the first century with Israel's and Jerusalem's destruction in AD 70, not global chaos and judgment.

- No future antichrist—The antichrist was Nero, or some even say the spirit of first-century false teachers.

- No rapture—It's the same event as the second coming.

- No second coming at the end of an actual seven-year tribulation—The second coming either happened in AD 70 (invisibly in the air) or will happen at some undetermined point in the future at the conclusion of a symbolic millennial reign of Jesus.

- No literal reign of Jesus in a millennial kingdom—His kingdom is now, and spiritual, not physical. The number 1,000 merely symbolizes a long period of time.

- No restoration of Israel, physically or spiritually—Instead, the church is the new Israel (Matthew 21:43; Galatians 3:28-29).

- No Armageddon—This as an allegory describing the fact that God always defeats His enemies.

So, the preterist's Revelation deals with Israel alone and not the world. Its events were local and not global. They were symbolic and representative, but not literal and actual.

Preterist Problems

What preterism fails to understand is that Matthew 24:29-31, which describes signs of the Son of Man's coming, has not happened yet. According to Jesus and Revelation, His return will be *visible*, and will include angel sightings along with great supernatural glory (Matthew 16:27-28; Revelation 1:7). If preterism is correct, then we are moving in time *away* from Revelation, not *toward* it.

Jesus also said there would be great persecution in Jerusalem that would cause His disciples to flee prior to His second coming (Matthew 10:23). This also has not happened in the way Revelation describes. An alternative view interprets "this generation" in Matthew 24:34

as referring to the generation living at the time of these prophesied apocalyptic events.

Also, the majority of the New Testament was written to help believers live between the first and second comings of Jesus. If He is already come, then what are we looking forward to? There is then no blessed hope that Paul tells us to look for (Titus 2:13). His admonitions to do so would have only lasted a few years since he wrote this verse in AD 65 and Jerusalem was destroyed in AD 70. This view nullifies much of the New Testament. Further, Satan is clearly not bound as Revelation 20 says he will be. And finally, why would Jesus's first coming be literal and physical, but His second coming be nonliteral and spiritual? This view cannot adequately explain the cataclysmic judgments of Revelation or the book's relevance to Christians today.

Historicist View

This view, which began around the twelfth century, sees Revelation fulfilled throughout a panorama of church history. It employs (and requires) a heavy dose of symbolism and allegory in order to reach its conclusions. However, as we survey church history in the last 2,000 years, we do not see any of Revelation's events occurring. Therefore, this view has not gained much traction due to its faulty foundation and unsustainable claims.

Timeless View

This view says that Revelation is nothing more than a verbal painting representing timeless truths—purity, hope, righteousness, sin, evil, retribution. But if this is true, how are we to make sense of the rest of the New Testament and the words of Jesus in Matthew 24? Was Jesus merely speaking in metaphors and symbols? That's not how His words were interpreted at the time. Or how do we reconcile the fact that the prophecies regarding Jesus's first coming were fulfilled literally and not figuratively? With this view, how could anyone confidently know what any of Revelation's symbols, metaphors, and word pictures mean? The timeless view makes interpreting prophecy like trying to nail Jell-O to the wall. It is a view, however, that blends in well with postmodern, progressive Christian thought, redefining concrete spiritual truths and turning them into helpful "life lessons."

One major problem with this view is that it generalizes and spiritualizes the Word of God. The Bible, though not primarily a book of history, certainly contains much historical data. Every time the Bible speaks about a historical event or person, it is eventually proved to be accurate. Contemporary archaeological discoveries continue to support the biblical record.

The point? Revelation describes detailed historical events that haven't happened yet. That's what prophecy actually is—history written in advance. The Bible is not an enigmatic book of ethereal poetry but a historic, literal record of truth. And its prophecies deal with specific persons and events, not mere symbols of spiritual truths.

The Futurist View

If Revelation's judgments didn't happen in AD 70, haven't been played out in history thus far, and are not mere allegories, symbols, or representative truths, then only one option is left to us—Revelation's events are still future. I believe the futurist view best explains this apocalyptic book, primarily because:

1. It employs the literal method of interpretation that we use to understand the rest of Scripture. This keeps our interpretive method consistent and our understanding of the Bible clear.

2. The world has never seen anything like what is portrayed in the book of Revelation. Chapters 6–19 have certainly never happened yet.

Therefore, if Revelation is future, and all past prophecies have been fulfilled literally, we can safely conclude that this book's prophecies will also come to pass just as the Bible describes.

Is There Any Reign in the Forecast?

We now turn our attention to the prophesied future reign of Jesus, that is, if and when there will be an actual millennial kingdom upon the earth. Specifically, what is the millennial kingdom? When does it occur? Has it already occurred? Or could it be happening now?

Let's begin with the basics. The word *millennium* means "one thousand." The word itself, like many other doctrinal terms we use, is not found in the Bible. However, we do see the truth of the millennium clearly taught. In Revelation 20:1-7, we see this number (1,000) repeated six times in seven verses. This repetition is meant to communicate a key aspect of Jesus's future kingdom. But what does it mean? There are three views concerning the 1,000-year reign of Jesus Christ.

Amillennialism

The prefix "a" means "no." Therefore, with amillennialism, there is no earthly reign of Jesus in a literal 1,000-year kingdom. His kingdom instead exists spiritually and in our hearts. The number 1,000 is symbolic and refers simply to an extended period of time. Amillennialism sees Satan being bound at the first coming of Jesus. However, one look at our world quickly dismisses this disbelief. Amillennialists do believe Jesus will return one day to judge humankind, but not following a seven-year tribulation. But if Jesus is currently reigning in the hearts of His people (as amillenialists claim), it would appear He is doing a poor job.

This view spiritualizes Scripture, interpreting prophetic passages and numbers as symbolic. This has been the predominant view of the Roman Catholic Church, the Greek Orthodox Church, and many Protestant denominations, such as Presbyterianism. It was also the view of Augustine, John Calvin, and Martin Luther.

Postmillennialism

In this view, Jesus Christ returns to the earth following a "millennium" consisting of a golden age of godliness that Christians have ushered in through the gospel's global influence. Postmillenialists see Christianity becoming so prevalent on the earth that Jesus will eventually be welcomed back to end the millennium and inaugurate eternity. This view sees the kingdom as *now*, but leading to the eventual return of Jesus.

However, if it is true that Christians are to bring about the kingdom on the earth through our worldwide influence, then we are failing miserably, because evil and wickedness are ruling the day. We are becoming more like the days of Noah, not more Christianized. Also, we have a long way to go before bringing in the kingdom because some four billion people on planet Earth have not yet heard the name of Jesus Christ.

Premillennialism

The premillennial position states that Jesus will return to the earth at His second coming *prior* to establishing a literal 1,000-year reign upon the earth. This belief sees Christ's millennial reign in a future era, during which Satan is bound, according to Revelation 20:1-9. Premillennialism was the predominant view among the early church fathers, among whom were Clement of Rome, Barnabas, Ignatius, Polycarp, Tertullian, and Justin Martyr. Premillennialists believe, along with those with differing eschatological views, that God is sovereign and ruling over and superintending all things at all times, including now. The difference is that they see a clear distinction between the nature and extent of His reign in this current age and His rule in the future millennial kingdom. Christ's reign in that day will be overt and obvious.

Defending Premillennialism

I believe the premillennial view is the one best supported in Scripture—for several reasons. Keep in mind that how you understand and interpret the 1,000 years is determined by how you understand and interpret the rest of Revelation. Like traveling a road leading to a particular destination, your hermeneutics (method of interpretation) will lead you to a particular general understanding of the Bible. How you begin determines where you end up. Again, I see the most effective and accurate interpretive method to be the literal, grammatical, historical, cultural, and contextual method. I believe this is how the Bible was meant to be interpreted and understood. Practicing this method, any studious believer can grasp the meaning of Scripture, from Genesis to Revelation.

With that in mind, here are seven reasons I believe that Jesus Christ will return a second time prior to establishing a literal 1,000-year rule upon the earth.

Reason 1—Premillennialism best fulfills God's promises to Abraham and David.

In the covenants Yahweh made with these men, specific promises were made.

- He promised Abraham that he would be the father of a great nation (Genesis 12:2). That promise was literally fulfilled.

- He also promised Abraham that He would bless him and that through him all the nations would be blessed (Genesis 12:3). That promise was also fulfilled literally.

- He promised to give Abraham and his seed specific boundaries of land (Genesis 12:1; 15:18-21). King Solomon came close to enjoying the fulfillment of this promise, but he never reigned over *all* the land God promised to Abraham (1 Kings 4:21). Israel has not yet ruled over these promised land boundaries, and therefore this prophecy would appear to be unfulfilled. I believe it will see its completion in the millennial kingdom.

- God promised David that his descendant would reign on his throne forever (2 Samuel 7:12-16). Three times in this passage God uses the word "forever," indicating the per-petuity of His reign. This prophecy, applied to Jesus in Luke 1:31-33, Acts 1:6-7, and Matthew 19:28, has also not yet been fulfilled because He is not currently ruling from David's throne (Hebrews 12:1-2).[3] However, at His second coming He will take His rightful place on this throne (Acts 15:15-18).

Reason 2—Premillennialism is consistent with the resurrections of Revelation 20:1-6.

The word *resurrection* (Greek, *anastasis*) is used 41 times in the New Testament to refer to a literal, bodily resurrection. It does not make sense that tribulation saints would be resurrected to reign with Jesus in some sort of symbolic 1,000-year kingdom. It also doesn't stand to reason that those unbelievers who died in the tribulation would be *physically* resurrected to be judged following an *allegorical* 1,000-year period. If the resurrection and judgments are actual, then it follows that the millennium would be as well.

Reason 3—Premillennialism was the belief of the early church and endured for the first three centuries after Christ's first coming.

Among the early church fathers who held this view were:

- Papias—bishop of Hieropolis, a companion of Polycarp, and a disciple of the apostle John (who wrote Revelation); Papias also cites the apostles Andrew, Peter, Philip, Thomas, James, John, and Matthew as being advocates of a premillennial position[4]
- Ignatius—first-century bishop of Antioch
- Polycarp—disciple of the apostle John
- Justin Martyr (AD 100–164)—wrote of the 1,000-year reign in his *Dialogue with Trypho*

- Irenaeus—bishop of Lyons (AD 120–202) and also a disciple of Polycarp

It wasn't until Augustine (AD 354–430) and his spiritualizing of the kingdom that the amillennial view gained prominence in the church (Luther, Calvin). Prior to this, the idea of amillennialism was associated with heretical, nonliteral approaches to Scripture.[5]

Reason 4—Jesus Christ's first coming was literal, physical, and to the earth.

Because of this precedent, there is no compelling interpretive or theological reason to believe His prophesied second coming and reign won't also be literal, especially since that's what Scripture seems to clearly state (Revelation 19:11-21; Isaiah 2:2-4; Daniel 7:13-14; Zechariah 14:4,9).

Reason 5—Premillennialism fits the most natural reading of the last days prophecies of Revelation 19–22.

Either Jesus's return, future reign on the earth, the great white throne judgment, and eternity are literal and real, or they are symbolic, figurative, or only take place in an unseen spiritual realm. The only other option is that you take all this language to simply refer to abstract spiritual truths. But according to John in Revelation 1:7, "every eye [on earth] will see Him." Physical eyes viewing a physical return. This would seem to naturally lead to a physical millennium. And referring to those in heaven redeemed during the tribulation, Revelation 5:10 says "they will reign upon the earth."

Reason 6—Premillennialism and the binding of Satan go hand in hand.

John's account in Revelation 20:1-3 provides us with meticulous details when describing the binding of Satan. If Satan's shackling was metaphorical, it would defeat the whole point of the language used. Instead, I believe an actual binding occurs here. John's language bears this out, using definitive words to describe specific objects, actions, places, and even a detailed time frame: angel, key, abyss, chain, hand, laid hold, bound, thousand, threw, shut and sealed the abyss.

The notion that the devil is somehow currently bound during Jesus's spiritual 1,000-year reign is absurd. Look around your world. Satan is still alive and well on planet Earth. He is still "the god of this world." Still "blinding the minds of the unbelieving." Still "the prince of the power of the air." Still "deceiving the nations" and still our greatest "adversary" (2 Corinthians 4:4; Ephesians 2:1-2; 1 Peter 5:8; Revelation 12:9).

Reason 7—Premillennialism involves a well-chosen, exact number given to John by Jesus Christ.

Many times throughout Revelation, John uses phrases that refer to more general or undefined time periods, such as "a little while longer" (6:11), "only a short time" (12:12), and even "short time," describing the length of Satan's release at the end of the millennium. If the 1,000-year number, repeated six times in seven verses (Revelation 20:1-7), isn't specific, literal, and exactly what God meant to say, then why repeat it so often? Why not simply say "a long time"? Why keep repeating a specific number when he could have used many other phrases to indicate an unspecified amount of time?

When we read Revelation, Jesus also reveals to John other precise numbers that are literal and exact, such as: "one hundred and forty-four thousand" (7:4; 14:1), "two witnesses" (11:3), "two hundred million" (9:16), "twelve hundred and sixty days" (11:3; 12:6), "seven thousand" who die in an earthquake (11:13), "ten horns and seven heads" (13:1), and a "third angel" (14:9). Why use numbers to communicate vague and symbolic concepts? Why can't God simply mean what He says?[6]

There is more we could say as to why all of Revelation should be understood literally, grammatically, and contextually. But to many prophecy experts and Bible scholars, these seven are convincing reasons why premillennialism is the best understanding of Jesus's second coming and His reign upon the earth.

There are reasons, of course, why other theologians hold the various views they do regarding the millennium. My purpose is not to demean them or demonize their views, but to present them (and evaluate them) so you can know what's out there. This way you are not uninformed or confused.

When Will the Rapture Take Place?

I realize that some of this is heady stuff, and frankly that's one reason why some Christians avoid the subject. But let's tackle one more huge topic before closing this chapter.

In my book *Wake the Bride*, I devote two chapters to defending the biblical basis for the rapture and how Scripture says it will happen.[7] I won't take the space here to revisit that treatment of the subject. Rather, what follows stems from the belief that there is going to be a rapture of the church. Put succinctly, the doctrine of the rapture teaches that at some future time, Jesus Christ will return for His bride, snatching her away to heaven, and sparing her Revelation's wrath. Simple as that.

But not so easy to swallow for some.

As with the topic of the millennium, there are differing views as to the existence, nature, and timing of this rapture.

The Midtribulational Rapture

This view states that Jesus rescues the church at the midpoint of the tribulation, or three-and-a-half years into that seven-year timespan. This halfway point marks the beginning of the *"great* tribulation," an intensifying of the suffering and judgment on the earth due to God's wrath.[8] In this scenario, the rapture coincides with the seventh trumpet of Revelation 11, which they also claim is the same trumpet of 1 Corinthians 15:51-52. To "midtribbers," the first six trumpets of Revelation 8–9 do not yet signify the great tribulation.

And yet, when we read of the seal and trumpet judgments in Revelation 6–9, it appears this period of great tribulation has most certainly already begun—famine, one-fourth of the earth's population killed, earthquakes, meteors, tectonic catastrophes (Revelation 6:15-17). This, to some, would indicate a major flaw in this view.

If there is a rapture at the midpoint of the tribulation, then it clearly fails to rescue the bride from the "wrath to come," as God's wrath has already come!

Further, placing the rapture at the exact midpoint of the seven-year tribulation removes all imminency for the Lord's return. The New Testament teaching that Jesus could return at any moment (imminency) is part of what feeds our hope and fuels our motivation to remain pure (1 Corinthians 1:4-8; 16:22; 1 Thessalonians 5:4-6; Titus 2:12-13; 1 John 3:1-3). The seven-year tribulation officially begins with the signing of a peace treaty between the antichrist and the Jews (Daniel 9:27; 2 Thessalonians 2:3-4). A countdown of 42 months (midpoint) would lead one right to a date for the rapture, which no person can know. With this view, you can almost set your watch to the timing of the rapture. But date-setting is unscriptural and never plays out. Thus, it should always be rejected.

Nowhere in Scripture are we given any prior countdowns, dates, or specific signs marking the return of Jesus at the rapture. By contrast, Jesus told His disciples that during the tribulation they actually *are* to look for signs, such as the abomination of desolation (Matthew 24:15), followed by the rise of false Christs (Matthew 24:23-26), and culminating with *the* sign of the Son of Man (Matthew 24:30).

The Posttribulational Rapture

Though there are some elements of agreement between views regarding the rapture and tribulation, their contrasts in timing could not be more different. The posttribulational view places the rapture at the conclusion of the tribulation. Therefore, Christians will be forced to endure all the divine judgments God pours out on humanity during this horrible, seven-year season. Here, the rapture and the second coming occur essentially at the same time, with Jesus raising the dead in Christ, snatching up the living, and then immediately continuing His descent toward the earth to engage the Armageddon campaign. We, the church, make a quick U-turn and go right back down to earth where we came from. It makes the two prophesied events virtually simultaneous. And yet in Revelation 19, there is no mention of a rapture or of saints being resurrected.

Mark Hitchcock writes,

> If God has miraculously preserved the church throughout the entire tribulation, why even have a rapture? Why bother? It's inconsequential. The Lord won't be delivering us from anything. There's really no purpose in it. Pretribulationism gives meaning to the rapture: if Christ comes before the tribulation, His coming is filled with purpose. He is rescuing us from the wrath *to come*[9] (emphasis added).

If either the mid- or posttrib views are true, why didn't Paul at least hint at this when giving comfort to believers in 1 Thessalonians 4:13-18 or 2 Thessalonians 2:1-7? Further, a person holding to a mid- or posttribulational rapture cannot in good conscience say Jesus could return at any time, since its timing is essentially revealed in their views. If we are currently *not* in the tribulation (which we are not), then according to these views we can say with certainty that Jesus is definitely not coming back for at least another three-and-a-half years, or perhaps seven or more years from now. This sort of knowledge concerning the rapture's timing is nowhere found in the New Testament. Further, enduring God's tribulation wrath removes Scripture's promise of deliverance through the rapture.

The Prewrath Rapture

This view claims the rapture actually happens five-and-a-half years into the tribulation. The prewrath position hinges upon a specific point when it is claimed God's wrath begins in Revelation. They arrive at this understanding based upon separating the judgments of Revelation into "man's wrath" and "God's wrath." They say God's wrath is not poured out until the sixth seal is opened in Revelation 6:12.[10] So somewhere between the sixth and seventh seal the rapture occurs.

However, Paul prophesies in 1 Thessalonians 5:1-3 that the world will be saying "peace and safety" immediately preceding "the day of the Lord" (or the tribulation judgments). If the rapture occurs where the prewrath claims it will, the world can hardly be characterized by peace and safety since it will have just suffered earthquakes, meteors, blood moon, global disturbances, and earth's inhabitants clamoring for shelter under rocks and in mountains to hide them from the awful wrath of the Lamb (1 Thessalonians 5:3; Revelation 6:12-17). There's plenty of horror and dread at this point, but no peace and safety to be found.

The Partial Rapture

This is by far the most untenable view, for it claims that *multiple* raptures occur throughout the tribulation. Here, a person's rapture is based upon their degree of faithfulness and obedience. Like getting into lifeboats on a sinking ship, not all go first, but eventually all do go. One of the many problems with this view is that it ignores the verses that indicate that everyone in the church participates in the rapture (1 Corinthians 15:51-52; 1 Thessalonians 4:14). According to Scripture, *every person* who is "in Christ" will be raptured (1 Thessalonians 4:16-17). Additionally, there is only one future rapture event recorded in the Bible (1 Thessalonians 4:13-18). There is also no indication of a hierarchy of salvation or of rapture deliverance in the body of Christ. Everyone who is saved is fully saved and qualified by Jesus's blood sacrifice to be delivered from the wrath to come. Obedience isn't the qualification for inclusion in the rapture. Salvation is. Besides, the Body is not raptured in pieces but as a whole. Rewards for faithfulness and obedience are given at the bema, which occurs in heaven following the rapture.

This view appears to stem from a legalistic add-on to the rapture doctrine, possibly in an attempt to motivate obedience through fear.

The Pretribulational Rapture

I have saved the best for last. This understanding of the rapture places it *before* the tribulation and *before* God's wrath is poured out on earth and its inhabitants. I believe the pretrib position is the one most supported by Scripture. It is not a view of convenience or of escapism, since suffering has always been a reality for believers, and persecution of Christians is ongoing in the world today, just as Jesus and Paul warned (John 15:18-23; 2 Timothy 3:10-12). In the pretrib view, life's tribulations cannot be avoided, but *the* tribulation can be. There are at least seven reasons why I and many others believe the pretribulational rapture most accurately represents what Scripture teaches.

The Promise of Jesus (John 14:1-13)

Jesus's wedding analogy was intentional here. He promised His disciples that after leaving them He would return one day to take them to His Father's house. This is precisely what happens with the rapture and what is happening right now, as Christ is preparing a place for us prior to His imminent and highly anticipated return.[11]

The Prophecies of Paul (1 Corinthians 15:50-58; 1 Thessalonians 4:13-18)

Paul encouraged the Thessalonian believers by telling them that before the day of the Lord arrives, Jesus Christ would personally return in the air to resurrect those believers who had previously died, and then immediately snatch up His bride to meet Him in the clouds. This event is clearly distinct from the second coming of Christ that we see in Revelation 19. In one, He returns *for* the church (rapture), while in the other He returns *with* the church (second coming).

The Pattern of Scripture (Genesis 6–7,19; 1 Thessalonians 1:9-10; 5:9-10; Revelation 3:10)

Believers are never promised exemption from trouble, suffering, or persecution. We are, however, promised exemption from God's wrath, be it apocalyptic wrath here on the earth or eternal wrath in hell (Romans 8:1). The Bible is filled with stories of suffering saints. But we are *not* destined to endure God's fury in any form. He rescued Noah prior to global judgment. He rescued Lot prior to raining down His wrath on Sodom and Gomorrah. This is testimony to the character of God and His commitment to spare His children from divine retribution. And He has also promised His church that she will also escape the coming tribulation wrath.

The Portrayal of Revelation

When we survey the book of Revelation, we see the word *church* mentioned 19 times in chapters 1–3. Then, much later we see the church portrayed as returning from heaven with Christ in Revelation 19, and then mentioned once again in chapter 22. However, noticeably absent in chapters 5–18, the chapters that describe God's wrath and tribulation, is *any* mention of the church. The bride of Christ simply does not reside on the earth during this terrible time. Though people will certainly become Christians during the tribulation, they will be slaughtered for their faith. But the bride is simply not there.

The Presence of Saints in Heaven

I believe the 24 elders mentioned throughout Revelation represent the church.[12] Every time we see them in that book, they are in heaven and worshipping before God's throne (Revelation 4:4,10; 5:5-6,8,11,14; 7:11,13; 11:16; 14:3; 19:4). The best explanation for the church to be missing during the tribulation and present in heaven during this time is that she has already been raptured.

The Purpose of the Seventieth Week of Daniel

Though individual Jews and Gentiles are one in the church, I also see a clear distinction between the church and national Israel. As has already been established, God has made specific prophecies to Israel that are fulfilled neither in the church nor in history. One of those prophecies is the "seventieth week" of Daniel (i.e., the tribulation). This prophecy specifically concerns Jews and Israel, not Gentiles (Daniel 9:24-27). And since the church had no part in the previous 69 weeks, it therefore stands to reason that she will not participate in the seventieth week, which is the tribulation.

The Preparation of the Bride

All throughout the New Testament the church is exhorted to make herself ready for the return of Jesus Christ. And although this return cannot be predicted, it *can* be anticipated. Paul went to great lengths to let New Testament believers know that the Lord's coming was imminent, meaning it could happen at any time. Therefore, a spirit of expectation was nurtured in the early church. Only a pretribulation rapture sufficiently explains this expectancy. If we knew when the rapture was going to occur (midtrib, posttrib), we could simply set our timers and wait for it. But because it could happen at any moment, we are motivated to always be pure and prepared (1 John 3:1-3).

Position Yourself

If Revelation has already occurred, then it is basically a book of history. It is no less the Word of God, but more like Joshua, 1 Kings, or Acts. If the events portrayed in the Bible's last book have somehow previously been fulfilled in the first century or throughout church history, then Revelation is more symbolic (and mysterious) than anyone realized. If Revelation merely depicts—through word pictures, metaphors, allegories, and symbols—timeless truths that apply to every age, then it becomes something to ponder, but not so much to anticipate.

But if we understand the last prophetic book of the Bible literally, then it must be pointing toward a future time in human history.

As we have seen, the doctrine of eschatology has a huge impact not only on the way we see the future but on the way we view reality today. If Revelation is still future, then it is a major gamechanger for our Christian lives. Because there are diverse views regarding the rapture, tribulation, and millennium, many Christians conclude that these doctrines must not therefore be essential or even that important. That's why a lot of churches simply avoid the subject altogether, leaving their sheep to fend for themselves in a pasture of ignorance, confusion, and irrelevance. This is tragic, and a further indication of the bride's current condition.

I do not believe it is essential for us all to agree on every point of eschatology in order for us to effectively function as the body of Christ. There are many godly men who hold divergent views on this subject. That doesn't mean there isn't a true and scriptural view or that we should detour around this doctrine because of our disagreements. But we should also never allow our views on the end times to create division or disunity in the body of Christ.

I once served on a church staff for ten years with five men, four of whom were premillennialists and one who strongly held to the amillennial position. Though we had healthy dialogue and even joked with one another regarding our positions, our difference of opinion on eschatology never once detracted from our great love for one another or our common mission together.

I encourage you to read others' works on the millennial kingdom and the rapture. But most of all, I encourage you to search the Scriptures for yourself and to come to a studied conclusion. Find a position and back it up with Scripture. If you do this, you'll neither be ignorant, confused, nor apathetic. Instead, you will clearly understand how relevant these doctrines are in your own life.

Chapter 8

Investigating "Prophecy Apologetics"

End-Times Evidence for Skeptical Minds

Worship God! For it is the Spirit of prophecy
who bears testimony to Jesus.
REVELATION 19:10 NIV

We live in an age where everything is amazing, but nobody is impressed. It's an era where accelerated advances in technology, travel, and medicine have catapulted us into a wonder-filled world. And yet this seems ordinary to us. The Internet alone may be the greatest technological advancement in human history, expediting personal interaction, vastly increasing our access to knowledge, and stimulating global economics. And with the explosion of online shopping, we can buy what we want without ever leaving the couch. In an instant, we text, talk, and send pictures and videos from our smartphones. What used to take days and weeks via snail mail now takes but a few seconds.

Today, about half of the world's population has access to the Internet, and thus, access to everything it provides.[1] And in first-world countries like America, nine out of ten people are regularly online. Things our parents' and grandparents' generations could not conceive are now commonplace realities. Concepts that just a generation ago would have been considered almost supernatural, we take for granted. Today's generation of young people has never known life without cellphones or the World Wide Web. These modern tools are the paved roads and running water of their ancestors' world.

And yet, no one today is amazed by these things. On the contrary, we're used to them. We expect them. And we're no longer impressed by them.

In the Ozark Mountains where I live, the night stars shine with brilliance against the backdrop of the charcoal sky. One reason God placed the stars in the heavens was for a visible testimony to His existence, grandeur, and majesty. Psalm 19:1 declares,

> The heavens are telling of the glory of God;
> And their expanse is declaring the work of His hands.

Charles Spurgeon referred to the stars as "God's traveling preachers" because they provide evidence of His majesty each evening in their journey across the sky.

But no one looks up at the stars anymore. We know they're there, but they no longer captivate us with awe. We are no longer enthralled by the wonder and worship God's creation once inspired. We don't look up and ponder the Almighty's greatness because we're too busy looking down at our smartphones or our computer screens.

Humanity is experiencing the death of the "Wow!"

If modern technology and the ancient universe no longer captivate or amaze us, then why should anyone be impressed with Bible prophecy? Why should the claims of an antiquated religious book change anyone's mind? About anything?

No "Apologies" Necessary?

In Bible history, God used tangible evidence to authenticate Himself to mankind. With Noah, He gave the sign of the rainbow as a promise to never again flood the earth with water (Genesis 9:12-17). To Moses, He gave tangible, supernatural signs to validate his claims that it was the Lord who would deliver the Jews from Pharaoh (Exodus 3–14). For Elijah, He showed up with fire on Mount Carmel to outduel the prophets of Baal and their absentee god (1 Kings 18). Jesus Christ healed the sick, raised the dead, and worked miracles to authenticate Himself as the Messiah. For the early church, God verified their message of salvation through Jesus with signs, wonders, and changed lives (Acts 2–3).

But as the New Testament canon came to a close, we saw the rise of a new apologetic from God. Since then, His primary authenticating proof of Himself has not been dreams, visions, supposed trips to heaven, or divine healings—it has been His *Word*. Even Jesus, the greatest miracle worker of all time, rejected the proposition of someone returning from the dead as convincing confirmation of the afterlife, hell's reality, and our need for salvation (Luke 16:27-31).[2] The parable of the rich man and Lazarus teaches us that miracles alone are not what ultimately convinces the human heart. For Jesus, the Word was enough.

Peter's defense of Christianity on the day of Pentecost was an appeal for his countrymen to believe Bible prophecy (Acts 2:14-36). He used the same presentation method of prophetic evidence to Jews gathered at the temple after the lame man's healing (Acts 3:12-26). Stephen's sermon before the high priest and the Sanhedrin was a historical walk through the Old Testament (Acts 7:1-53). Paul often employed the prophetic Scriptures to prove that Jesus was the Christ (Acts 13:13-41). When attempting to persuade pre-Christian pagans, he employed human reasoning along with quoting their own poets in order to establish common ground and to build a bridge to his audience. However, his presentation crescendoed with the proclamation of God as Creator and Jesus as Judge, "having furnished proof to all men by raising Him from the dead" (Acts 17:16-31). This was another convincing fulfilled prophecy (Psalm 16:10; Isaiah 53:5,8,10; Matthew 12:40; 16:21; Mark 9:9-10; John 2:19-22; 10:17-18; 11:25-26; Acts 2:22-32).

These are some biblical examples of God's "apologetics." The Greek word *apologia* means to "make a verbal defense." It often referred to a courtroom context when an attorney would present a reasonable, convincing case. The New Testament uses the word to describe Paul defending his testimony before the Jewish leaders (Acts 22:1), defending himself before the Roman governor Felix (Acts 25:16), defending his apostleship (1 Corinthians 9:3), and defending the gospel he preached (Philippians 1:7,16). It's also used of Christians "always being ready to make a defense" of the hope that is in them (1 Peter 3:15).

But one undeniable principle emerges out of all these biblical occurrences: God's Word is the proof people need.

It is clear that many other pre-evangelistic methods and supportive apologetics contribute toward the credibility of Jesus and the Christian message. The apologetics of logic and philosophy appeal to human reason. Scientific apologetics help prove the Bible's accuracy. Historical apologetics demonstrate the Bible as a reliable historical document. Literary and textual apologetics help document the Scriptures as being consistent over many thousands of years.

These apologetic areas are all useful with various audiences. And the testimony of a changed life can also be a powerfully persuasive tool in romancing a sinful heart toward the Savior.

But two factors must accompany all these areas of apologetics if a person's mind is to be fully convinced and their heart truly changed. They are:

1. Truth from God's Word about Jesus
2. The Father and the Holy Spirit drawing someone to salvation

Apart from these two supernatural sources, intellectually convincing a person of the reliability of Scripture or of the reality of Christ is ultimately an exercise in futility. This is not in any way to suggest that the aforementioned areas of apologetics are unnecessary, for they all play a major role in building bridges to minds and hearts. But where the rubber meets the road is when the Word of the infinite God and His Holy Spirit do what only they can do—persuade a person to accept God's truth, recognize their desperate need for salvation, and trust Jesus's ability to save them (John 3:3-6; 6:44,65; 15:26; 16:8-11; Romans 3:10-12; Ephesians 2:1-2; Titus 3:5).

While on a walking tour of Colchester, England, a few years back, our pastor guide showed us the remains of what is believed to be the oldest church building in all of Great Britain, dating to the third century. Standing on that crumbled wall foundation, my heart was grieved. What remains of that church seems emblematic of the Christian church in England today. Empty cathedrals echo the silence of sermons once preached in them. Abandoned church buildings are now restaurants or shops. Many congregations have dwindled to just a few aged members. Though God is still at work in that history-rich country, the church there is but a shadow of what she once was.

I see a similar slow death occurring in our churches here in the United States. Many congregations are dwindling and even dying. Simultaneously, our greatest weakness is how little we impact American culture. Our society has become much more secularized in the past 50 years, and increasingly ungodly. Evangelism and apologetics are like two wings of an airplane, and in our culture the church needs both to fly. Try to evangelize in the twenty-first century and you'll instantly realize the great need to be equipped in this area. Because of this, I see at least six reasons why Christians must be better equipped with a convincing biblical apologetic.

Reasons for a Biblical Apologetic

1. We Live in a Fallen World

The human heart is darkened and blinded (John 3:19; Romans 1:21; 2 Corinthians 4:4). Adam's fall affected every aspect of our being—physical, mental, emotional, spiritual, relational. This is one reason why truth is such a contentious issue today. Barna Group research shows that 64 percent of adults and 83 percent of teenagers believe moral truth depends on the situation you are in.[3] In other words,

Americans base truth on their feelings, not on facts. Reason is dying because humanity is very broken.

Further, we can no longer assume people have any previous or basic knowledge about God, the Bible, Jesus, or salvation. What people do know may likely be tainted or outright false. That's why we are often forced to begin with the ABCs (Always Been a Creator) of apologetics as Paul did in Acts 17. Reason has been usurped by emotion.

2. Our Faith Is Being Attacked and Ridiculed

In America, Christianity is being marginalized in the media, schools, academia, and in the sciences. Christians are portrayed as repressive, bigoted, and "homophobic." Our morality has gone the way of the VCR and the home landline, having become all but obsolete. We have been told to get past our faith and join the human race. Therefore, we desperately need equipped Christians to penetrate every segment of society with the ambiance and influence of the gospel.

3. Christians and Churches Have Misrepresented the Message of Jesus

Confusion is created when "rock star" pastors build kingdoms for themselves or disqualify themselves morally. Some attempts to reach new generations through "relevance" have backfired, producing even more resistance to the gospel. Many churches have strayed from the truth, becoming more self-help seminar centers than disciple-making communities of faith. We get off point and off message. Some Christians tarnish Jesus's reputation through living in sin or simply settling for mediocrity instead of the victorious, abundant life He promised (John 10:10; 16:33; Romans 8:37).

4. Many Christians Do Not Know Why They Believe What They Believe

In October 2012, the Pew Forum on Religion and Public Life reported, "The fastest growing 'religious' group in America is made up of people with no religion at all, and one in five Americans is not affiliated with any religion...The survey found that the ranks of the unaffiliated are growing even faster among younger Americans. Thirty-three million Americans now have no religious affiliation, with 13 million in that group identifying as either atheist or agnostic."[4]

They're called the "Nones."

America's Research Group found in 2009 that the majority of our churched kids drop out of church by college age.[5] Almost 50 percent say no one has *ever* taught them how to defend the faith. We teach some of the "what" of God but not so much the "why." So when the world asks them "why?" they have no defense, and thus lose confidence in their faith.

Because of this lack of equipping in churches, we are producing and perpetuating a generation that is practically ineffective as it relates to the kingdom of God. And with no filter through which to sift the world's values other than their own feelings, they embrace unbiblical philosophies, beliefs, and values. And just as Paul predicted, they are tossed back and forth by every wind of doctrine (Ephesians 4:11-15).

5. Ours Is a Reasonable Faith

The good news is that there is both a "what" and a "why" to our faith that contradicts neither true science, reason, logic, or history. God created reason and the human mind. And humanity was fashioned with the capacity to discover and comprehend logic and process deduction. Only when the mind is marred by sin, self-centeredness, and rebellion do we lose the ability to properly think and reason (Romans 1:18-32; Titus 1:15-16).

6. The Times in Which We Live

As we discern the day, it is clear that history is being groomed for Revelation. Storm clouds are gathering, and now, more than ever, we must point others to the Ark of salvation. Fortunately, prophecy helps us do just that.

So, clearly today there is a need for believers to be able to defend the faith.

Jesus Really Is Amazing

Jesus Christ is the centerpiece of history. He is also the source of our salvation. What He accomplished through His death provides the basis upon which the Father can expunge all our sin from heaven's record (Ephesians 1:7; Hebrews 7:25; 1 John 2:1-2). Sometimes the simple telling of the gospel story is all it takes to convince a sinner of his or her need for salvation.

But there are also historical and prophetic facts that underscore His person and work. He is the ultimate apologetic. Consider that:

1. Jesus Christ was a real person. The Christ-myth has no historical basis whatsoever since there are numerous secular, nonbiblical sources that also document Jesus's historicity. Among these are the Roman historian Cornelius Tacitus (AD 56–120), the Jewish historian Flavius Josephus (born AD 37), Suetonius (born AD 69), Pliny the Younger (born AD 61), and Thallus, a Samaritan-born historian.[6]

2. Jesus Christ claimed equality with God. Far above merely posturing Himself as a rabbi or prophet, Christ clearly and repeatedly declared Himself to be equal to God (Matthew 26:63-66; John 5:16-24; 8:19,54-59; 10:22-39; 14:1-9; 18:4-6). He forgave sins (Mark 2:1-12), accepted worship (Matthew 14:22-33; John 20:26-29), and predicted His own death and resurrection (Matthew 16:21; 17:22-23; 20:17-19; 26:1-2,31-32). And either His claims were true, or they were not. What does the evidence say?

3. Jesus Christ fulfilled the Old Testament prophecies regarding the Messiah. For example:

• He would be born to a virgin (Isaiah 7:14; Matthew 1:18-25).

- His physical place of birth was named (Micah 5:2; Matthew 2:1-6; Luke 2:4-7).

- He would ride into Jerusalem on a donkey (Zechariah 9:9; Matthew 21:1-11).

- He would be beaten and abused (Isaiah 50:6; Matthew 26:67-68; 27:24-31).

- He would be betrayed with money (Zechariah 11:12-13; Matthew 27:1-10).

- His hands and feet and side would literally be pierced (Psalm 22:16; Zechariah 12:10; John 19:34-37).

- He would die with criminals (Isaiah 53:12; Matthew 27:38).

- His bones would not be broken (Psalm 34:20; John 19:31-36).

- Though killed with wicked men, His grave would be associated with a rich man (Isaiah 53:9; Matthew 27:57-60).

- He would be physically raised from the dead (Psalm 16:10; Matthew 28:1-7).

These are impressive facts. But wait—there's more.

What Are the Odds?

More than 300 prophecies were fulfilled at Christ's first coming, and every one of them literally and exactly as predicted.[7] This is further evidence of why the Bible should be interpreted and understood plainly. And what is the mathematical probability of *one person* fulfilling *all* those prophecies? First, the chances of one man fulfilling just 8 of those 300 prophecies is 1 in 100,000,000,000,000,000! That's 1 in 100 *quadrillion*.

Professor Peter Stoner famously estimated that if you took 100 quadrillion silver dollars and spread them out over the state of Texas, they would cover the entire land mass (that's 268,597 square miles) two feet deep! Then mark just one of those coins and toss it into that mass of money, mixing it thoroughly. Blindfold a man and have him walk the whole state, stop at any point, reach down and randomly select one coin. Stoner says the mathematical chances of that man choosing the marked silver dollar on the first attempt are the same chances one man could fulfill *just 8* of those Messianic prophecies.[8]

Stoner further calculated the odds of any one man fulfilling 48 of those prophecies to be at 1 in 10 to the 157th power. That's 10 with 157 zeros after it. The math is so mind-blowing that the professor was forced to illustrate it using the miniscule example of the electron. Smaller than atoms, it would take 10 quadrillion (10 with 15 zeros after it) electrons laid side by side to equal one inch. Counting at 250 electrons per minute, 24 hours a day, it would take you 19 million years to count them.[9] That's just one inch of electrons. The number of electrons in Stoner's calculation would measure over ten inches, theoretically taking you 190 million years to count them! Blindly locating the one marked electron in this massive number is a probability beyond our ability to imagine.

The professor wisely concludes, "Any man who rejects Christ as the Son of God is rejecting a fact, proved perhaps more absolutely than any other fact in the world."[10]

Jesus existed. Concerning this there is no reasonable doubt or credible evidence to the contrary. And because of His claims to deity, He cannot simply be an ordinary man, a great teacher, or a good example of peace and love. The same Jesus who washed the disciples' feet also said He was God. The same Christ who encouraged us to "love your enemies" also made prophecies concerning a wrath-filled apocalypse. The Rabbi who told His disciples, "Do not judge so that you will not be judged," also warned of a coming day when He Himself would bring judgment on the earth and on hardhearted skeptics (Matthew 7:1-2; 24:29-41; 25:31-46).

Same Jesus.

Christ made claims that were grand and glorious. And yet, they were not the rants of a delusional or demented religious cult leader. If He was God in the first century, then He still is today (Hebrews 13:8). Therefore, His prophetic Word remains valid and trustworthy. If He is still dead, then the book of Revelation is nothing more than an apocalyptic dream of a deranged old man. But if He is alive, then Revelation is real. That's because everything Jesus said about Himself and His future return stands or falls with the resurrection (1 Corinthians 15:1-19). But Christ validated Himself as God through His authenticating miracles and His resurrection. Further, His redemptive work on the cross was also confirmed by His resurrection.

Because of these proofs, His second coming is *preauthenticated and guaranteed.* If His resurrection happened (Matthew 28; John 20), then His prophesied second coming is 100 percent guaranteed (Zechariah 14:4; Matthew 24; Revelation 19).

Prophetic Previews

The Bible's Track Record

The Bible has a 100 percent accuracy rate with regards to prophecy. Everything the Scripture has ever predicted would happen has come true, exactly as predicted. God's Word is batting a thousand. Never missed. Not even once. So, Scripture's track record is reliable and undeniable.

Jesus, Paul, James, and Peter spoke quite a bit about the last days of the church age and of the end times themselves (Matthew 24; Luke 21:5-36; 1 Timothy 4:1-3; 2 Timothy 3:1-5; James 5:1-3; 1 Peter 1:20-21; 2 Peter 3:3-13). In the last week of His earthly ministry, Jesus's disciples asked Him privately,

> "Tell us, when will these things happen, and what will be the sign of Your coming, and of the end of the age?" And Jesus answered and said to them, "See to it that no one misleads you" (Matthew 24:3-4).

He then launches into some of the apocalyptic vision we read about in Revelation 5–19, telling them that the end times will closely resemble "the days of Noah" (Matthew 24:4-37).

So if all of Revelation 5–22 is still future, then it is also, by default, *prophetic*. Therefore, the question becomes, Do we currently see anything happening in our world that *foreshadows* those prophecies? Anything that may be precursors, tremors, or, to use biblical imagery, "birth pangs" leading toward the end of days? Are we seeing signs of the end times? What's happening right now that tells us we are getting close to the fulfillment of Bible prophecy?

Stage-Setting Realities

I believe there are some present, stage-setting realities that indicate we are closer than ever to the return of Jesus Christ. I see these prophecies-in-the-making not only as apocalyptic, but also apologetic. They stand as compelling reasons why any open-minded, thinking person should consider the Bible and Jesus Christ.

1. Bible prophecy tells us that in the end times the Jews will return to occupy the Holy Land.

The nation Israel *must* be reborn and living in their homeland for the events of Revelation to unfold (Jeremiah 30–31; Ezekiel 34:11-24; 37; Zechariah 10:6-12). Much of Revelation's events and timing hinge on the existence of the nation Israel. This prophesied gathering is a *process* and has been going on for about 130 years, beginning with the Zionist movement in the late 1800s (Ezekiel 37:1-14). The Jews are the only exiled people group to remain distinct, despite being scattered to more than 70 countries for more than 2,000 years. Egypt, Assyria, Babylon, Persia, Greece, and Rome all conquered them, took their land and people captive, and dispersed them throughout the earth. They have been persecuted throughout the ages, and yet Abraham's sons and daughters have somehow survived.

Then on May 14, 1948, Israel officially became a nation again. No one could have seen this coming, except perhaps a student of Bible prophecy. And now, here we are. Today, more Jews live in Israel than at any time in 20 centuries (6.3 million).[11] The Jewish people are coming home, just as the Old Testament predicted and the book of Revelation portrays.

To a reasonable mind, the fact that Israel as a nation is once again living back in the land is a fulfilled prophecy. It is *the* super sign of the end times, and also a convincing apologetic as to the reality of what else the Bible says is coming.

2. Bible prophecy states that Israel will be invaded by a coalition of nations from every direction (Ezekiel 38–39).

The goal of these allied armies is to eradicate Israel from the earth, wiping the Jews off the map of history (Ezekiel 38:10-16). Gog is named as the specific leader of the invasion, with the remaining proper names referring to geographical locations. (The participants in this unprovoked aggression were listed in chapter 6, along with their modern-day identities [Ezekiel 38:2-6,15; 39:1-2].)

Keep in mind, there was never a recorded invasion like this against Israel in the Old Testament and could not have been for the last 2,000 years because there was no Israel! This battle happens sometime between the *physical* rebirth of Israel as a nation (Ezekiel 37) and its *spiritual* rebirth (Ezekiel 40–48), so sometime between 1948 and Christ's future physical reign on earth.

So where does that leave us? What do we know for sure?

- Israel is now in the land.
- Some of the Muslim nations surrounding Israel would love nothing more than to exterminate the Jewish people.
- Scripture predicts this war will happen.

Ezekiel 38–39 (Gog/Magog War) was written 2,600 years ago and is immediately preceded by Ezekiel 37 (regathering of Israel to the land). So the chronology is as follows:

- Israel is reborn and returns to the land.

- The Jews are living at peace and securely in the land.
- An invasion occurs involving the nations prophesied in Ezekiel 38–39.
- God defeats Israel's enemies supernaturally.

As stated earlier, I believe this battle will not occur until some-time after the antichrist signs a peace treaty with the Jews, which officially marks the beginning of the seven-year tribulation (Daniel 9:27; Matthew 24:15-16; 2 Thessalonians 2:3-4). This treaty likely accounts for the peace and security Israel will experience just prior to this war. That points to a possible invasion scenario in the early months of the tribulation.

The fact that this 2,600-year-old prophecy could be on the verge of fulfillment is more than a lucky prediction by Ezekiel. Prophets don't get lucky. They get it right. Every time. Apart from divine inspiration, how could Ezekiel have possibly known that in the last days these Jew-hating nations would be Israel's surrounding neighbors?

3. Bible prophecy tells us antichrist's peace treaty will make it possible for the Jews to rebuild their temple in Jerusalem and resume the Old Testament sacrificial system (Daniel 9:27; Matthew 24:15; 2 Thessalonians 2:3-4).

Remember, there hasn't been a temple in Jerusalem since AD 70. They've gone 20 centuries with no homeland, organized nation, or temple. Now they are a nation once again and are moving back to the land. In 1987, an organization called the Temple Institute was formed in anticipation of a rebuilt temple. They have already fashioned sacred temple vessels and priestly garments according to exact Old Testament specifications, and have drawn up blueprints for construction. They are sponsoring classes to train young men for the priesthood. This is more than a hope for these Jews. It is their mission. But they are powerless to begin construction until some agreement is made concerning the controversial Temple Mount, the area on which the Jewish temple stood and which is currently under Muslim control. They are simply waiting for a way (peace treaty) to secure the real estate and begin construction.

The apologetic? The Bible prophesies that a Jewish temple will be rebuilt during the tribulation (Daniel 9:27; 2 Thessalonians 2:3-4; Revelation 11:1-2). Today, for the first time since AD 70, an organization stands at the ready, prepared to begin the construction and reinstitute the Jewish sacrificial system. This process could easily begin with the stroke of a pen belonging to a proclaimed peacemaker and world leader. The fact that this is currently even a remote possibility is more than noteworthy. It is a flashing neon sign of prophetic significance.

4. Bible prophecy tells us that in the end times there will be a revived Roman Empire/United One-World Government (Daniel 2:36-45; Revelation 17:9-10).

Satan's goal has always been to rule the world, beginning with Genesis 11 and Nimrod. The Bible describes a revived Roman Empire that will form in the end times. Though we do not know which ten nations will comprise this one-world government, the current European Union (EU) or something resembling it *could* eventually fulfill the prophecy of such a global coalition. Antichrist will lead this multinational confederacy.

Throughout history, many military leaders and kings have sought to rule the world, or at least a big portion of it. The person the Bible calls "the man of lawlessness...the son of destruction" will succeed in this ambitious endeavor (2 Thessalonians 2:3). Capitalizing on world chaos following the trauma brought on by the rapture, this son of Satan will spearhead a multinational alliance to govern global affairs.

Today, many nations are irreversibly bound together economically. We are racing toward globalism and international interdependence. In other words, the world is becoming one, and this is by Satan's design, a counterfeit kingdom mimicking Messiah's future reign. Antichrist will provide the glue that unites the nations together in earth's final days. Technology, language, the decline of nationalism, communications, and the need for peaceful cooperation all bring this prophecy closer to potential fulfillment with each passing day. This prophecy is not far-fetched, and given the right circumstances, it could materialize within a matter of months.

5. Bible prophecy tells us antichrist will require every person to take a "mark on their right hand or on their forehead" (Revelation 13:16-17).

This is often called the "mark of the beast" or "666." The Greek word *charagma* ("mark") was used in the first century to describe an emperor's image on a Roman coin or a stamp or seal on an official document. In Revelation, it's an identifying representation enabling a person to buy and sell during antichrist's reign. Capitalizing on a post-rapture panic and the economically crippling judgments that follow, the beast of Revelation could bring the entire world into submission with promises of "peace and safety" (1 Thessalonians 5:3). He will gain control over commerce and who is permitted to buy and sell (Revelation 13:17). And John writes that "all who dwell on the earth will worship him" (Revelation 13:8).

No one knows exactly what this mark will be, but we do know it will brand all those who worship the antichrist. It will also be a survival necessity at this point in the tribulation. A cashless society is not an unrealistic proposition, as many nations already process the majority of their economic transactions wirelessly and electronically.[12] Forty-five percent of America's transactions are now cashless.

Today, checkbooks are virtually nonexistent among young adults. Online purchases, debit cards, and cash app transfers from smartphones are now the norm. The mark of the beast will simplify and streamline these economic transactions. Further, the need to be united will be critical in that day. The technology for this mark of the beast is already here, whether some form of radio frequency identification (RFID) or another, perhaps more primitive method. All we're waiting on is for a world crisis to make it absolutely necessary and for the "good of humanity."

6. Biblical prophecy tells us that when Christ returns, His feet will land on the Mount of Olives (Zechariah 14:4; Acts 1:9-12).

His touchdown will cause a massive, violent earthquake, splitting the mount in half east to west, causing it to move north and south. In 2004, *NBC News* reported a three-year study by the Geological Survey of Israel, confirming this very area to be at imminent risk of an earthquake. Their conclusion was based on the discovery of a fault line running east to west...*right through the Mount of Olives!*[13] So how could Zechariah, writing 2,600 years ago, have possibly known about this future fault line? This is another example of Scriptural evidence of the certainty of future prophetic fulfillment. Had Nostradamus or some medieval soothsayer predicted a future earthquake on the Mount of Olives and this recent geological evidence confirmed it, he would be hailed as a clairvoyant, psychic, or an oracle of the ages. Why not believe the same amazing predictions of those whom the Bible calls "prophets"?

Bottom line: The Mount of Olives is going to split in half when Jesus's feet touch down there. Of this you can be certain.

7. Bible prophecy says the last days would resemble "the days of Noah."

I briefly touched on this earlier, but Jesus predicted one of the end-times signs would be a striking similarity to the days of Noah (Matthew 24:37-39). Rewind to that awful era in history, and we observe four distinguishable characteristics rising out of the waters of that day: (1) pandemic godlessness, (2) unrestrained immorality, (3) worldwide violence, and (4) a surging global apostasy.[14]

Welcome to America.

But it's not just here. All across the world, nations have become more secularized, entrenched in paganism or atheism, or otherwise preoccupied with the worship of a false god or gods. The sexual tsunami that has breached our moral levees has spread so far inland that there is little chance these wicked waters will ever recede. The legalization and celebration of gay marriage, transgenderism, multiple genders, and the unbridled sexuality that permeates our culture is a sure indication that heaven's judgment is unavoidable (Romans 1:18-32).

Further, through wars, regional skirmishes, genocides, terrorism, barbaric death cults, a spirit of lawlessness, mass shootings, and the daily global slaughter of the unborn, we are sufficiently bleeding the ground red.

Finally, Christianity is being marginalized more today than perhaps at any time since the first century. Christians across the globe are being martyred for their faith. The society that once held high biblical morality and values is now hanging and crucifying in social media those who espouse such values. Even within the church, core Bible doctrines are being downplayed, redefined, and in some cases dismissed and denied. They are being pushed aside, dumped into the ash heap of theology in order to make room for more relevant, positive, and expedient topics. "Preach the Word" has been replaced with "Make 'em feel good!" Christians, churches, ministries, schools, colleges, and entire denominations are falling away from the faith, just as Jesus and Paul prophesied (Matthew 24:4-12; 1 Timothy 4:1-?; 2 Timothy 3:1-5; 4:1-4; Titus 1:10-16).

All these stage-setting signs are more than coincidences, anomalies, or interesting facts. I believe they incarnate a convincing apologetic to thinking, open minds. They are tangible and they are documentable.

In addition to these,

- Expect to see more global economic and geopolitical chess pieces being slowly moved into place by a God who is sovereign over history.

- Expect to see further ripple effects from the legalization of homosexual marriages. Read Romans 1:18-32 and see if it doesn't describe the world around you in those verses. Once a depraved humanity's perverse fleshly desires are sanctioned and unleashed into culture, a landslide of immorality cannot be far behind. The radical gay agenda will expand, demanding equal rights and recognition of adult-minor sexual relationships, multiple marriage partners ("throuples"), and a host of other perversions.

- Expect to see a continued defense and justification of the slaughter of the unborn, a blatant and unapologetic disregard for the sanctity of human life. Like the days of Noah, as we continue squeezing God out of every segment of society, education, culture, and our national consciousness, this and other types of violence will only increase.

- Expect to see increased persecution of Christians across the world and at home in the days leading up to the rapture. Jesus said, "If the world hates you, you know that it has hated Me before it hated you...If they persecuted Me, they will also persecute you" (John 15:18,20).

- Expect to see more global conflict, sword-rattling, and the threat of war. As Jesus prophesied, "All these things are merely the beginning of birth pangs" (Matthew 24:6-8).

These things do *not* mean the rapture, Revelation, and tribulation will happen tomorrow, but they do signify that the conditions are right for the end-times storm to reach the catastrophic stage. Dark clouds are gathering as we speak. Do not be naive or ignorant. If you are a thinking person, you have to at least admit the world is heading toward something, and that something isn't good. What we are seeing take place in our world was prophesied thousands of years ago in Scripture. God's Word was written to give us a heads-up on history so we could know how to prepare.

Here Am I

With all these prophetic previews in the making, how prepared are you to defend Scripture's prophecies? Or how well do you know your own faith? I'm not referring to your personal belief in Jesus, but rather *the* faith once for all delivered to the saints. It's this faith for which you and I are commanded to "contend earnestly" (Jude 3).

Paul reminded us that the lost cannot believe unless they hear from "a preacher" (Romans 10:14). *You* are that preacher. You are His message-bearer, a divinely appointed truthteller to a generation lost in sin and cyberspace. You are Christ's ambassador to the world. His bride, the church. His representative. There are millions more of you than there are professional pastors, speakers, and authors. And if this army of spiritual soldiers fails to invade culture with Jesus's truth and love, who will? God's strategy to validate His reality and truth to the world requires convinced and transformed people just like you. Committed, equipped, and motivated disciples.

Our core message remains the same for two millennia—Jesus Christ died to save sinners. You are a sinner. You need Jesus. Trust in Him for forgiveness and salvation.

And yet, in today's post-Christian culture, we quickly discover that people have legitimate questions about our God and how to reconcile Him with the troubling times in which we live. Yes, God's Word is eternal and powerful (Isaiah 55:11-12; Matthew 5:17-18; 2 Timothy 3:16-17; Hebrews 4:12). But merely lobbing gospel grenades of truth over the church walls at a depraved culture and expecting change won't cut it. Just quoting Bible verses won't cast a magic spell on someone. If they believe the Bible is a manmade book, then rattling off a verse will likely be ineffective. You will need to lay a foundation for the gospel by demonstrating *why* the Bible is not only unique and trustworthy, but also worthy to be considered supernatural.

And that's when you suddenly find yourself doing apologetics.

In this world climate, there are no unimportant areas of apologetics. God uses them all, from logic to science to life apologetics (character, kindness, mercy, connecting in relationships). Making a defense of your faith means being set apart for Jesus, ready to speak with knowledge, confidence, personal experience, and love (1 Peter 3:15). And that's something every growing Christian can do.

Obviously, some people are so closed-minded that you couldn't jackhammer a mustard seed of truth into their minds. They wouldn't believe even if you produced a video of Jesus rising from the dead. Some, to be sure, are so in love with their sin that they stiffen at the mere suggestion of abandoning it. The door to their minds and hearts has been slammed shut, locked and bolted from the inside. They are not open to hearing about Jesus or having a conversation about God, salvation, or the reality of prophetic times in which we live. They defend their right to sin and are openly defiant against the God of the Bible. Further, they enthusiastically applaud sin in others.

Some of today's skeptics mock the fact that Christians have been talking about the second coming of Jesus and the end times for centuries. "Guess what?" they scoff. "The world is still here, and Jesus is a great big no-show!" (see 2 Peter 3:3-9). Others, because of additional intellectual roadblocks, immediately reject God's truth. However, some will give the evidence an audience in their minds. And if you've established a trust relationship with them, they are much more likely to listen.

Prophecy apologetics is necessary in an age where we see the stage being set for Revelation. It helps Christians apply biblical discernment to today's events in order to share with a world looking for answers.

Undoubtedly, we find ourselves at an unprecedented crossroads in human history. At no previous point have the events of Revelation been more suitable for a near future fulfillment. Many of Scripture's future realities are beginning to materialize before our eyes. These emerging signs are convincing proof that God and His Word are real, dependable, credible, and unavoidable. Therefore, they must be taken seriously.

For reasons we've explored in this chapter, Bible prophecy is certainly an apologetic for our time.

With the fulfilled prophecy of the rebirth of Israel in 1948, it's as if a logjam of prophetic precursors were freed and now are flowing downstream toward their appointed destination in history. None of the signs we've discussed were viable prior to the reestablishment of the nation of Israel. And yet today all of them are undeniable stage-setters to coming realities.

The point of prophecy is Jesus Christ (Revelation 19:10). We must do more than just connect ancient prophetic dots to modern-day happenings. Prophecy without Jesus is interesting, maybe even convincing. But when we use prophecy to point others to Him, it becomes full-on transformational.

And right now, our world desperately needs the change that only He can bring.

Chapter 9

Building Up the Body of Christ

The Barnabas Principle of Prophecy

Instruction does much, but encouragement everything.

Johann Wolfgang von Goethe

American culture has become saturated with a spirit of hostility and animosity. In our government, partisan political attacks perpetually fuel a war of opposing values and ideas. As a result, the rift between parties grows wider each week. Could we be a country any more divided politically than we are right now? But it's not just in government. Our nation's news outlets have devolved into tabloid journalism, reporting the news largely through the filter of a political, social, or moral agenda.

For the rest of us, social media has become America's new town hall, where conversations are made, rants are posted, opinions shared, and debates held. What transpired in past generations around the general store Buck stove, barbershop, or beauty parlor is now openly displayed for the world to see on sites like Facebook and Twitter. This forum is fast filling up cyberspace with vitriol and verbal assaults. Today, you must tread lightly if you step onto the digital highway, for you may quickly find yourself in the path of oncoming traffic. Post a belief or opinion, and you could suddenly find yourself the target of Internet hate mail, online bullying, and even character assassination. Reveal your political persuasions, conservative views, or biblical morality online, and you are almost guaranteed to find yourself in the crosshairs of dozens of snipers who unload a magazine of verbal malevolence. Yesterday's back alley mugging is today's online attack.

This is the world we live in. The World Wide Web provides hate-filled hearts the ability to throw stones from behind virtual walls. Of course, it's much easier to tear someone down or to attack them than it is to dialogue with them or to build them up. And when it comes to actual encouragement, it's easier to simply do nothing at all.

In the church, however, it's a markedly different story. It's not so much that we are verbally destroying one another like they do out in the world. Rather, we are not intentionally building one another up in the way Scripture prescribes. When a human body functions properly, the body is strong. And part of having a healthy body is when each of its members does its part to support others in the body as a whole. Feet support legs. Hands help the mouth and eyes.

So how is this principle supposed to work in Christ's body today? How many churchgoing Christians regularly and purposefully build up others in the body? Can you recall a specific time in the last month when another believer has said or done something to you that strengthened and encouraged you and your faith and relationship with Jesus Christ?

Filling Up and Fueling the Fire

I wonder what percentage of discourse among believers is marked by shallowness instead of spirituality? Are we content with secular conversations, or do we pursue scriptural ones? Do we limit our language to temporal topics, or do we ever dialogue about eternity? Of course, we should talk about earthly things. We have to. We are earthbound for now, and earthly things are a part of our lives. But could it be that our relationships are lacking the kind of empowering interaction that marked the early church? We may be good at *relational* encouragement, but that doesn't necessarily mean we are *spiritually* encouraging one another. We can successfully make people feel better about themselves, and yet still not strengthen them in their relationship with God. For these reasons, biblical encouragement just might be the lost art of the church.

In God's Word, we observe that spiritual encouragement was to be the norm among believers and not the exception. After describing the ungodly as "the ones who cause divisions, worldly-minded, devoid of the Spirit," Jude admonishes, "but you, beloved, [build] yourselves up on your most holy faith" (Jude 19-20).

Notice this edification takes place in the environment of our *faith*. This kind of encouragement builds us up in our spiritual lives. Paul commanded the Ephesian Christians to "be filled with the Spirit" (Ephesians 5:18). The Greek verb he uses here—*plēróō*, "to be filled"—contextually means to "strongly influence." And what is the by-product of the Holy Spirit's influence on a Christian? Paul gives us the answer in the very next verse, "speaking to one another in psalms and hymns and spiritual songs, singing and making melody with your heart to the Lord" (5:19).

To the Colossians, he declared a similar principle with almost verbatim results: "Let the word of Christ richly dwell within you, with all wisdom teaching and admonishing one another with psalms and hymns and spiritual songs, singing with thankfulness in your hearts to God" (3:16).

The first thing we should observe here is that allowing the Word of God to richly fill our minds and hearts is synonymous with allowing God's Holy Spirit to influence us. The reason for this, according to the apostle Peter, is that it was the Holy Spirit who inspired the Word of Christ to be written (2 Peter 1:20-21)! So when the Spirit fills us, or when we get into the Word, there is a *spiritual* outcome. Within a community of faith where the Word of God is faithfully taught, there should be an organic overflow of heart worship and of imparting biblical wisdom to one another through teaching and admonishing.

Vertically, in the body of Christ, we receive truth from God and then respond with worship back to Him. Horizontally, we minister to fellow believers, building each other up. This is not solely the responsibility of the pastors or other leaders, but rather the calling of every member in the body of Christ.

While in college, I was a part of a discipleship group led by a Campus Crusade for Christ staff member. After several months of meeting together weekly, one of our members complained, "Why do we always have to talk about the Bible all the time?" To which our leader responded, "Charles, it's simple. Spiritual people talk about spiritual things."

For Christians, spiritual encouragement should be the rule, not the exception. If you don't have a church or a group of fellow believers where this is a reality, then perhaps you should be the spark that starts the fire.

Side by Side

I believe biblical encouragement is one of the greatest needs in the church today. We are a nation of consumers, and the American church is made up of those consumers. Consequently, it's very easy to simply show up on Sundays expecting to get something and to be served in some way. But that is only part of why we gather each week. We also come together for the purpose of strengthening and building up one another. And why is this spiritual encouragement so desperately needed among Christians today?

1. We Need Encouragement Because Life Is Hard

We live in difficult days and uncertain times. The world is more volatile and unpredictable today than it has been since the Cold War. Economic crises, the threat of Islamic terrorism, the powder keg of instability in the Middle East, the violence in our streets, the racial tensions and moral decadence that are tearing apart the fabric of our nation...all these combine to create a spirit of anxiety.

For Christians, many fear for their children and grandchildren as they are daily thrust into a pagan culture of self-worship and immorality. It's not just hard to make a living these days. It's hard to make a *life*! It can also be difficult to persevere and run this long-distance race of faith that is required of us. Therefore, we need regular doses of hope in the midst of this tempest.

2. We Need Encouragement Because the Devil and the World Are Against Us

Satan is the god of this world (John 12:31; 2 Corinthians 4:3-4). He is the prince of the power of the air, and the one who dictates the ungodly values and worldly thinking so prevalent worldwide (Ephesians 2:2). This satanically controlled worldly system is set up in such a way that humanity must conform to it or pay the price of being persecuted by it (John 15:18-23; Romans 12:2). The temptation to simply go with the flow and be pressed into the world's mold with its values and priorities can be intense. That is why God commanded us to be fully devoted to Him as a deterrent to falling under the world's influence (Romans 12:1). And if all this wasn't enough, the Bible tells us that our adversary also "prowls around like a roaring lion, seeking someone to devour" (1 Peter 5:8). Even so, he can be resisted by those who are firm in their faith and who are *encouraged* by the example of other believers (5:9). We must encourage one another to stay in the fight and persevere!

3. We Need Encouragement Because the Lord Hasn't Returned Yet

The apostle Peter prophesied 2,000 years ago, "In the last days mockers will come with their mocking, following after their own lusts, and saying, 'Where is the promise of His coming? For ever since the fathers fell asleep, all continues just as it was from the beginning of creation'" (2 Peter 3:3-4).

Let's face it, even as Christians there are times when we wonder why the Lord hasn't already returned. I mean, how bad do things really need to get before He descends from heaven with a shout? Today, perhaps no doctrine of the Christian faith is so mocked and scoffed at more than the rapture, specifically, the pretribulational rapture. This belief has come under fierce attack even by those within evangelicalism. But no matter what your view is on the return of Jesus, the fact remains that He has still not arrived. And because some in our culture think that's because He's *never* coming back, this is confirmation to them that our faith is a farce. Admittedly, this fact can create tension in our faith, and even doubt. Because we live in a post-Christian culture filled with vocal skeptics, we can expect even greater ridicule and mockery concerning His return up until the actual day it happens.

As an encouragement to us, however, Peter does explain at least one reason why Jesus has not yet returned, stating that God is patient toward the unsaved, "not wishing for any to perish but for all to come to repentance" (2 Peter 3:9). In other words, Peter says, "Don't mistake an unfulfilled promise made by Jesus to be an illegitimate one. The reason He hasn't returned is not because He can't or eventually won't, but because He is willing to give sinners another day to repent."

Like first-century believers, today's church is marginalized, ridiculed, mocked, and persecuted. We are no longer the mainstream. The moral majority has become the immoral majority. Therefore, the community of Christ must be our safe haven and a sanctuary from the arrows of the enemy and attacks of the world.

Bodybuilding with the Bible

But how does Scripture, specifically Bible prophecy, fit into this important admonition to encourage and build up one another in the body of Christ? As we have seen with prophecy, many Christians find themselves stuck somewhere between ignorance ("I have no idea") and fatalism ("God's going to do what God's going to do"). Neither are acceptable, biblical, or helpful.

Two of the biggest lies believed about Bible prophecy are (1) it isn't real, and (2) it isn't relevant to daily life. These myths are blown away by the truths we've covered in this book. Prophecy is not only real but also very convincing. And it's as relevant as any other doctrine in the Bible (2 Timothy 3:16-17). The confusion concerning how Revelation practically intersects with their lives leaves many Christians wondering just what to do with it. Is it nothing more than evangelical entertainment for prophetically curious minds? Or is it an actual blueprint for things to come?

I trust that what you've seen in this book convinces you of the latter. That said, we must remember that God did not record His truth so we could merely receive it and rest in it. There is also a sense of accountability that comes with that body of truth. We are responsible to share it, not only with the world but also within the church. This was Paul's admonition to Timothy, that he would find faithful men and pass on to them what he had heard from the apostle (2 Timothy 2:2). As my former seminary professor Howard Hendricks used to tell us, "Gentlemen, you cannot impart that which you do not possess." In other words, it is only what we have received from the Lord, through His Word, that we are able to share with others in the body. Shallow and immature Christians can only go so deep in their interaction with other believers. But those who are maturing and deepening themselves in Christ and His Word have something of greater substance with which to encourage fellow saints. Depth breeds depth.

In writing to the Romans, Paul told the strong to help those in the church who were weak, and that they should not merely please themselves. In other words, don't be consumers but givers of good to fellow Christians, to their "edification" (Romans 15:1-3; cf. Galatians 6:10). Then, in the next verse, he explains, "For whatever was written in earlier times was written for our instruction, so that through perseverance and the encouragement of the Scriptures we might have hope" (15:4).

It's clear from this passage that God's Word is a great source of hope. And perhaps no group of New Testament believers needed hope more than the Romans. They witnessed firsthand the paganism and persecution that flowed from Caesar's throne and the Roman Empire.

And how does the Scripture encourage us? Most everyone familiar with the Bible knows those verses that have become famous for being comforting and encouraging. Passages like: Psalm 23—"The LORD is my shepherd...even though I walk through the valley of the shadow of death..."; Joshua 1:9—"Be strong and courageous! Do not tremble or be dismayed, for the LORD your God is with you wherever you go"; and Matthew 11:28—"Come to Me, all who are weary and heavy-laden, and I will give you rest."

It's easy to see why verses like these have become so treasured and widely shared within the body. However, when thinking about comfort and encouragement, our minds may not immediately run to verses about end-times prophecy, right?

But why not?

Brick House

The Need for Encouragement

The Bible tells us "we are members of one another" (Ephesians 4:25). In other words, we are bound together by a common faith in the same Lord. We also share a spiritual DNA that sets us apart as the church or the "called out ones" (Greek, *ekklesia*). As it relates to encouragement within the church, God chose a unique word to communicate this important truth. It's the word *parakaleo* (*para*, "alongside," *kaleo*, "called"). The word primarily means to be called alongside someone for the purpose of comforting, admonishing, consoling, or instructing. It can also mean to be called to the aid of someone, to urge, exhort, encourage, or cheer them up.[1] This powerful word is used over 100 times throughout the New Testament with those meanings.[2]

Encouragement isn't simply complimenting someone regarding

their appearance or achievements. Biblical encouragement goes much deeper than that.

Several years ago, my wife and I founded a weekly youth ministry that met in our home. In time, we had around 40 teenagers invading our house every Wednesday night for dinner, and afterward discipleship and Bible study in the basement. Periodically, we celebrated what we called "Brick House Night." I had an old brick from an 1800s building that once stood in my hometown. My artist wife then painted the words "Build Up One Another" on one side of the brick. We explained to our group that bricks are made for the purpose of building things up, not tearing them down. We passed the brick around to anyone who requested it, and upon receiving it they had to choose someone else in the group and publicly praise and encourage him or her. The rule was that you couldn't compliment them about their beauty, academic or athletic accomplishments, or some external quality. Rather, you had to speak a word of biblical encouragement regarding their character or some other Christian quality they exhibited. The result was that we had a group full of highly encouraged young people! We later took that same brick with us to the church we founded in our historic neighborhood and introduced the "Brick House Principle" to adults. We could all use some more bricks in the church today, wouldn't you agree?

But the question remains, "How does this kind of encouragement relate to Bible prophecy?"

In Paul's teaching on the rapture in 1 Thessalonians 4:13-18, he laid out both the nature, imminency, and chronology of this glorious prophetic event. He then concluded with a climactic exhortation, "Therefore *comfort* one another with these words" (4:18).

How the Teaching About the Rapture Comforts Us

Paul could've ended this prophetic teaching in a multitude of ways. He could have said, "So be warned" or "And now you know" or "Isn't this awesome?" But, directed by the Spirit, he admonishes us to comfort (*parakaleo*) one another. And how does the truth about the rapture comfort us?

1. The prophetic rapture truth gives us confident hope that we will be reunited with those believers who have died ahead of us. This is the primary meaning of verse 18 in its context, related to the promise found in verses 13-15. The rapture will be a joy-filled reunion for those who are alive when it happens. And the comfort of knowing we will once again see our departed loved ones is simply indescribable. Can you think of someone right now you are looking forward to seeing again?

2. The prophetic rapture truth marks the "completion" of our salvation. Though we were saved from the penalty of sin at the moment we placed faith in Christ, we have not yet been fully delivered from sin's residual influence on us *or* its presence. However, the rapture will accomplish this, with the assurance that Jesus will transform us into His likeness and give us new, supernatural bodies fit for heaven's environment (1 Corinthians 15:51-57; 1 John 3:2). Every day we sin and fail the Lord. Every day we face temptation. And every day we are acutely aware of our fallen humanity. But the rapture brings an end to that long struggle with sin (Romans 7:14-25). Could anything be more practical than that?

3. The prophetic rapture truth finalizes Jesus's eternal purpose for choosing us—that we would "be with Him." Perhaps the deepest thought we could ever entertain is the idea that God loves us and actually wants to be with us. It boggles the mind and humbles the heart. And yet, according to Jesus and Scripture, this has been His desire since before the foundation of the world. The Son's goal of us "being with Him" is a theme running throughout the New Testament (Mark 3:14; John 14:3; 17:24; Ephesians 1:3-14; Philippians 1:23; 1 Thessalonians 4:17; 5:9-10; Revelation 17:14; 21:1-4). The return of Christ for the church achieves this goal. The rapture takes us to Jesus! This is one reason why it is called the blessed hope.

Paul had earlier commended the Thessalonian Christians for their repentance and faith toward God, and the fact that they were waiting "for His Son from heaven...who rescues us from the wrath to come [the tribulation period]" (1 Thessalonians 1:10).

He then reinforces this truth in chapter 5, stating this deliverance would occur *before* the "day of the Lord" (which again signifies the tribulation period): "For God has not destined us for wrath [the outpourings of His judgments during the tribulation], but for obtaining salvation [at the previously mentioned rapture] through our Lord Jesus Christ" (5:9).

And the practical "so what?" application of this prophetic deliverance truth? Paul again gives it to them in the verse that follows: "Therefore *encourage* [from *parakaleo*] one another and build up one another, just as you also are doing" (5:11).

In the rapture, there is both *consolation* regarding departed believers (1 Thessalonianas 4:13-15) and the *encouragement* that we will see them again (4:17). The truth about this reunion would have brought the Thessalonians great comfort, but Paul's emphasis is not just on the comfort they receive, but the comfort they give *one another*. The command, "comfort one another *with these words*" (4:18) can more literally be rendered "*in* these words." The power of our encouragement is found in the Word! What a powerful and pragmatic application of prophetic Scripture.

Paul's point earlier in the passage was that unbelievers have no such hope. They have no comfort. They possess no afterlife confidence. For them, facing death and eternity is a step into unknown darkness. The best the world can offer them are fairy tales and false hopes. For those without Christ, funerals are full of grief without relief. But for those who know Jesus and expect His soon return, a funeral is but a temporary separation. For us, it is never "Farewell," but rather, "Until we meet again."

Turn It Up!

The writer of Hebrews gives us further insight and motivation into this prophecy-related admonition:

> Let us hold fast the confession of our hope without waver-
> ing, for He who promised is faithful; and let us consider
> how to stimulate one another to love and good deeds, not
> forsaking our own assembling together, as is the habit of
> some, but encouraging one another; and all the more as
> you see the day drawing near (Hebrews 10:23-25).

The "day" in this context is the second coming of Jesus Christ, and
a key truth we learn from this passage is that we actually can "see" that
day approaching. This is not a justification for sensationalistic date-
setting, but instead puts into practice the discernment we discussed
in chapter 3. I believe the stage-setting signs of Revelation we saw in
chapter 6 are precisely the kinds of harbingers that enable us to "see
the day drawing near."

But it goes beyond being able to recognize the season of prophecy
we're in. Hebrews tells us there is a required response associated with
recognizing our last-days' existence. We must encourage one another
"*all the more*" in light of Jesus's approaching return. As we see the end
times dawning on the horizon, we are to dial up the encouragement
factor to the next level. We obviously do not know the precise *when*
of Revelation's coming events, but we can recognize the signs that tell
us we're in the ballpark. Today, we see the precursors to Revelation,
tribulation, and the second coming of Christ...and the rapture hasn't
even happened yet!

So what does that tell us? It is evidence suggesting we are in a season
where these things could soon take place. Just as it was for those believers to whom Hebrews was written, so it must be for the church today.
We must strengthen and build up one another during these last days.

Think about it. We spend all week out in a world that is decidedly anti-Christian. Many disciples across the globe are dying for their
faith while others are experiencing increasing hostility and persecution. For this reason, when we gather together as the body of Christ, it's
not "just another Sunday." Our assembling together must be an oasis
of encouragement and edification in a vast desert of discouragement

and opposition. A church family should be the safest, most loving, and most uplifting place on the face of the earth. It is there where our wounds are tended to, our minds challenged, our souls equipped, our relationships strengthened, our vision clarified, and our spirits inspired and motivated. Wouldn't it be great if every church functioned like this? Does yours?

Beloved, we are encouraged when we *know* something about prophecy (1 Thessalonians 4:13-18), and when we *see* something about prophecy (Hebrews 10:23-25). And what we see is the day of Jesus's second coming drawing near. And we know that prior to this we will be delivered. Jesus is coming for His bride! Perhaps now we can understand a bit deeper why the early church greeted one another with *Maranatha* or "Our Lord, come!" (see 1 Corinthians 16:22). This regular reminder of Jesus's imminent return was a truth that built them up and sustained their faith during hard times.

And this encouragement is just the tip of the iceberg regarding what Bible prophecy does for us. Of course, it *warns* us. It *informs*, *educates*, and *equips* us. But it also:

- Strengthens our faith in Scripture as we see past prophecies fulfilled and future prophecies coming into focus.

- Deepens our understanding of God's character and ways as we understand and accept His sovereign superintending of history.

- Nurtures proper humility, knowing that we are not in control of things.

- Motivates our mission to reach a lost world before God's patience comes to an end (2 Peter 3:9).

- Empowers us with courage and hope as we face these troubling times with Holy Spirit-infused confidence.

- Clarifies our current struggles and burdens, putting them into proper perspective. We realize they are temporary and "not worthy to be compared with the glory that is to be revealed to us" (Romans 8:18).

If the pretribulation rapture isn't true, then Paul would have repeatedly warned the Thessalonians (and believers throughout the New Testament) to "brace yourselves for the tribulation that's coming." Instead, his emphasis was on positive, uplifting encouragement in view of God's prophetic promises.

The "Tongue of Disciples"

Mark Twain wrote, "I can live for two months on one compliment." Tom Sawyer's author certainly understood the power of an encouraging word. It's a word spoken that uniquely fits the person and the moment. Instead of hurling bricks or shooting barbed arrows of discouragement, the word of encouragement breathes new life into the hearer.

Solomon, a man far wiser than Mark Twain, wrote, "How delightful is a timely word!" (Proverbs 15:23), and "Like apples of gold in settings of silver is a word spoken in right circumstances" (Proverbs 25:11). And Isaiah prophesied concerning the Messiah's earthly ministry, "The Lord GOD has given Me the tongue of disciples, that I may know how to sustain the weary one with a word" (Isaiah 50:4).

We need this language of encouragement on our tongues today.

Paul urged the Ephesians, "Let no unwholesome word proceed from your mouth, but only such a word as is good for edification according to the need of the moment, so that it will give grace to those who hear" (4:29).

If Mark Twain could fuel his life for two months on a simple compliment, why can't Christians supply and inspire one another with the substantive truths found in God's prophetic word? The answer is...we can!

When I was 13 years old, I broke my wrist in a bicycle accident. I was at a cousin's house at the time, and they immediately put ice on it as it was rapidly swelling to twice its normal size. I remember being so afraid since I had never broken a bone before. My aunt called my older brother, and he came and took me to the emergency room. My wrist was throbbing, pounding with excruciating pain. I was drenched in sweat and filled with fear. And the only thing I wanted to know was, "When is Dad going to get here?"

My young mind was consumed with anxiety over just how they were going to fix the bone that was protruding out of my wrist. We waited and waited for an orthopedic doctor to show up, and when he finally did, I became even more afraid over what he was about to do to me. All along, my big brother kept repeating, "Don't worry, Jeff. Dad's coming. Hang in there. He's on his way."

It seemed like I was in that emergency room for hours, but before long the curtain parted and I saw my dad's face. My pain did not go away, but my fears sure did. I knew I was going to be okay, because my daddy was there. And what kept me hopeful during my waiting time was my brother's strong encouragement, "Dad's coming, Jeff. Dad's coming." His were comforting words spoken at the right time. And in my frantic moment, those words flooded my young heart with hope.

Brothers and sisters, these troubling times we're living in are *our* moment. Many Christians are enslaved by fear. They are held captive by apathy, ignorance, mediocrity, and defeat. Their confidence is waning and their hope is weak. What they need is a *word*! And that word is the encouragement you can give them from *the* Word. In light of the prophetic season we're in, God's truth about the future gives us real hope in the right now. Because we see the day drawing near, let us be intentional about our encouragement and build up one another through our words and deeds. What will make the difference for us will not be happy thoughts, positive thinking, or a self-help sermon. No. For followers of Jesus Christ, it is His transforming truth that is the source of our survival and the fuel for our assured victory.

Use this secret key of Bible prophecy and open your own door of encouragement in the body!

Chapter 10

Preparing for Jesus's Return

Possessing a Certain Hope and a Pure Heart

*Looking for the blessed hope and the appearing of the glory
of our great God and Savior, Christ Jesus.*

TITUS 2:13

On a vast estate in Staffordshire, England, there stands a curious structure. Built sometime between 1748 and 1763, this stone edifice rises some 20 feet high and measures about 15 feet wide. Thick chiseled columns frame the huge tomb-like architecture. The centerpiece of this curiosity, known as the Shugborough Monument, is a large marble carving. On it is sculpted a depiction of a Nicolas Poussin painting called *The Shepherds of Arcadia*. But that's not the most interesting aspect of this peculiar monument.

Below this sculpted rendering are a series of mysterious letters: O U O S V A V V. Positioned slightly underneath them, and on either side, are two more letters, D and M. And therein lies the conundrum. No one knows what these letters mean. This alphabetic riddle has baffled some of the world's greatest minds for over 250 years. Hundreds have offered theories and explanations as to its meaning, but no one has yet successfully deciphered this cryptic text. The ten-letter chiseled inscription remains a secret, sealed within itself, its meaning hidden from humanity.

Some have interpreted the message as a love note, left there by the monument's builder, Thomas Anson, an architect and member of British Parliament from 1747 to 1776. Others have believed it to be a coded message of the Knights Templar, revealing coordinates leading to the location of the Holy Grail. Still other theories are more trivial in nature, claiming the letters are nothing more than an eighteenth-century riddle meant to puzzle future generations.

Today, the Shugborough estate is managed by the National Trust of England, whose staff say they are contacted weekly by individuals claiming they have finally solved this mystery. One such man is Keith Massey, a former USA National Security Agency employee and Arabic linguist. Massey says he has deciphered the cryptic code, claiming it corresponds to the Latin phrase "Oro Ut Omnes Sequantur Viam Ad Veram Vitam," which when translated reads, "I pray that all may follow the Way to True Life." Massey believes this is a reference to Jesus's words in John 14:6, "I am the way, and the truth, and the life."[1]

However, despite his assertion, the estate's management maintains the Shugborough inscription nevertheless officially remains "unsolved." Though the world may never know the precise meaning of these mysterious letters, there is no debate that this ancient inscription continues to confound linguists, code crackers, historians, and tourists.

The Prophecy Code

Many of the subjects we have discussed in this book are often viewed much like the Shugborough inscription. To many Christians today, the specifics of Bible prophecy are simply an unknowable riddle. An uncrackable code. An elusive enigma. A scriptural curiosity at which spiritual tourists pass by and scratch their heads.

But fortunately, as we have seen, Bible prophecy is not some unsolvable riddle. Instead, it is revealed truth God intended us to understand and believe. Admittedly, not every detail of Revelation's prophetic story is presently clear. It would be both irresponsible and also arrogant to claim full knowledge of how and when all the events of God's apocalypse will unfold. But make no mistake. Bible prophecy is not the spiritual equivalent of an ancient cryptic code. Rather, it's an integral part of the inspired revelation. It's not only *in* the Bible, but it makes up some 28 percent of all Scripture. And best of all, it was written for our benefit.

We've also seen that there is much more to know about prophecy than most Christians are willing to discover. In this book, together we've encountered the nature of prophecy, and revealed the biggest mistakes people make with it. We've learned how to develop biblical discernment, how to spot counterfeit truth and false prophets, and how to interpret prophecy. We have surveyed some of the major prophecies that remain unfulfilled, overviewed diverse end-times views, and seen how prophecy can be a convincing apologetic. And most recently, we've understood how it builds up and strengthens others in the body of Christ.

And yet, even with all this, I believe prophecy's greatest impact occurs when we personally apply it to our own relationship with Jesus. Thus, the real question becomes, "How should my life be different as a result of knowing Bible prophecy?" And here is where God seems to get specific and prioritize.

Though prophecy inherently conveys many benefits, perhaps none is so personal and practical as what we read in 1 John 3:2-3, "Beloved, now we are children of God, and it has not appeared as yet what we will be. We know that when He appears, we will be like Him, because we will see Him just as He is. And everyone who has this hope fixed on Him purifies himself, just as He is pure."

We saw in 1 Thessalonians 4 that a radical, supernatural transformation will occur when Jesus Christ descends from the sky, rapturing us to Himself. It is then that our conformity to the image of Christ will be complete (Romans 8:29). This has been His purpose all along, the predestined desire of God for His people. And He always finishes what He begins. As Paul declared, "For I am confident of this very thing, that he who began a good work in you will perfect it until the day of Christ Jesus" (Philippians 1:6).

However, in the time between His "good work" beginning in us and our "perfection" on that day, the Lord wants us to *prepare* and *purify ourselves*. This is our objective. Our mission and primary purpose. It's Christian living at its best. Could anything be any more practical than this?

Of course, every Christian experiences the tension between focusing our energy on the everyday responsibilities of life here on earth and looking forward to our blessed hope and eternal destiny. We live here, but we do not belong here. Our bodies are here, but our hearts are tilted toward heaven. As Paul wrote to the Colossians, "Therefore if you have been raised up with Christ, keep seeking the things above, where Christ is, seated at the right hand of God. Set your mind on the things above, not on the things that are on earth. For you have died and your life is hidden with Christ in God" (Colossians 3:1-3).

While our minds are on His priorities and values, we still have to take care of things down here. We walk in two worlds, don't we? And this is not an easy perspective to balance and maintain. But though the earth is not our home, God has nonetheless placed us here for a season and for a reason.

There is a well-known expression that states, "Some people are so heavenly minded that they are no earthly good," meaning we can become so preoccupied with spiritual things that we neglect earthly matters of importance. While I understand the intent of such a saying, I have rarely seen it in action. On the contrary, many Christians I've known have their affections and emotional roots so deeply entrenched and intertwined with the things of this world that there is little room for spiritual priorities. If we honestly evaluated our time, energy, and desires, we might discover that our lives are predominantly filled with temporal, trivial pursuits and worldly preoccupations. Some of this is due to the nature of life itself in the world we live in. But we can easily lose ourselves and get caught up in culture's current and swept out to sea. As Christians, we are by nature and calling countercultural to the flow of this world and its values, priorities, and desires. This requires us to make intentional choices based on a biblical mindset. We must choose to obey His mandate in order to break free from worldly priorities and agendas.

For believers, the first thing we typically neglect is the Bible. We can do church, fellowship groups, and even the occasional mission trip just fine. But if our enemy could place a spiritual roadblock anywhere, it would be in the path between us and God's Word. If he can keep us from Scripture, then he essentially cuts off our food source and weapon supply.

Additionally, we discover that our old sin nature stands in the way of our interaction with the Bible. Too often we are too busy or too lazy. We rationalize, finding reasons to avoid God's written Word, inventing a multitude of excuses. This is also true as it applies to Bible prophecy. However, this changes when we see how all of Scripture is profitable and practical (2 Timothy 3:16-17). Besides, what could be more natural than for a bride to prepare for her wedding day? Everything she does is with her wedding in mind. It is her life dream come true. Her ultimate red-letter day. Her highest priority and ambition.

Preparing yourself to meet Jesus Christ is a higher priority than loving your spouse and family or maintaining and managing your career. It's even of greater personal importance than reaching your world with the gospel. I realize that may not sound quite right upon first reading. But take a moment and contemplate this truth. It's not that evangelism is not important. It very much is. But of greater importance is the condition of our hearts and lives at the moment the Son of God appears. What good is our evangelism if our hearts are not pure and prepared for Him?

Don't you agree?

A few years ago, I was invited to be a guest on *Fox & Friends* regarding my book *As It Was in the Days of Noah*. Realizing I would be seen and heard by millions of Americans caused me to spend time poring over my notes in order to clearly articulate the book's message and respond appropriately to questions. I even consulted my wife about what I should wear. Though the interview lasted only a few minutes, I spent hours in preparation, making sure that my one chance to tell America about God's prophetic plan and the hope of salvation in Jesus Christ would not be wasted. I savored the privilege of being able to share God's truth on national television. Ultimately, my preparation paid off, and the interview went well.

But a national television appearance, no matter how important, pales in comparison to a Christian's appearance before the one Audience that really matters. Because we will all appear before Jesus, either at the rapture or at death, we must invest much time in preparing ourselves for that glorious moment.

How odd would it be for a bride to know very little about her future husband until her actual wedding day? And yet, with so much biblical illiteracy among Christians today, and so much misinformation about the Bible, theology, heaven, eschatology, and the person of Christ Himself, I fear Jesus's rapture return may catch a large percentage of believers off guard. Unless we devote time to God's Word and the nurture and spiritual development of our lives, the Jesus who comes in the clouds will be unfamiliar to us. Could it be that many professing Christians will not recognize Christ when He returns? Jesus himself warned that many who call him Lord and who claim to prophesy in His name, even casting out demons and performing many miracles, will be denied entrance to heaven because they did not actually *know* Him (Matthew 7:21-23).

Does the American church know Jesus Christ?

Truths that Transform

A key element in our preparation to meet Christ involves pursuing Him consistently by being saturated with His Word. There is no other spiritual discipline more needed today in the church than personally interacting with Scripture. Yes, you can pray. But pray what? And to whom? And how? Without the knowledge and equipping that comes from Scripture, we become functionally ignorant. We know enough to effectively speak "Christianese" in our prayers, but often lack fervency, depth and real knowledge (Colossians 1:9). Without an ever-increasing understanding of God from Scripture, our prayers grow stale, our faith remains stunted, and our lives become ordinary. But through the Bible, we keep learning who God is. Prayer, then, largely becomes the expression of our hearts based upon what we have gained from His Word. So unless we are immersing ourselves in the Scriptures, we cannot effectively know the God to whom we are praying. It's also in the Bible where we learn *how* to pray, and *for what* we should petition Him.

Bluntly put, if you're not in the Bible, you have become deceived into thinking you really know God. There is no substitute for time spent in the Word. Not a sermon, podcast, or this book. Rather, the more you get into *the* Book, the more familiar you will be with the Person you will see at the rapture or at the time of your death.

Can you think of a more relevant way of preparing to meet Jesus than this?

With that in mind, let's pull over and take in the biblical scenery God has provided for us in 1 John 3:1-3. Looking more closely at what John says in these verses, we discern four main truths.

First, we are children of God because of His great love for us (1 John 3:1). Salvation did not originate with our desire, but with God's. He chose us in Christ before the foundation of the world (Ephesians 1:4). Apart from His sovereign, choosing love, we would never seek God or find salvation (John 1:12-13; Romans 3:9-12; Ephesians 2:1-9). Never. You and I could no more become saved on our own any more than a rotting corpse in a graveyard could raise itself from the dead. He alone is the source of our salvation. As the psalmist proclaimed thousands of years ago, "Salvation belongs to the Lord" (Psalm 3:8).

But are we merely saved from sin by a cold, detached deity? No. Our God is personally and relationally attached to us. More than just our Creator, He is also our loving Father. And the love He bestows upon us before, during, and after salvation is truly immeasurable. The three most unbelievable words I have ever contemplated are, "God loves me." And sometimes I still find it hard to believe. Being a child of God is the greatest status a person can know. The absolute pinnacle of human experience.

Second, our future transformation is certain (1 John 3:2). John uses one of his favorite words here—*know*. Don't you love his confident language? He is not guessing or hoping or wishing. He is saying our assurance of salvation's completeness is greater than some positive mind trick meant to keep us happy. No. It is God's personal guarantee to us, backed up by the authority of His own Word (Romans 8:28-30; Philippians 1:6; 3:10-14). The word *hope* here (and throughout the New Testament) means "a confident expectation." We may wish for things that we want. But we *expect* the things we *know* are going to happen. This is not an entitlement mentality, but simply taking God at His Word. John adds, "*when* He appears" (3:2). Not "if" or "should He one day" appear. This too is a coming certainty. And when He does come, the beloved apostle declares, "we will see Him just as He is." Right now, we live by faith and not by sight (2 Corinthians 5:7). But when Jesus comes, in an instant our faith will be overshadowed by the reality of what we will see. No man has seen God in His glory (Exodus 33:17-23; John 1:18; 1 John 4:12), but at the rapture we will come face-to-face with the glorified Christ of Revelation.

Contrary to popular thought, death and taxes are not the only two certain things in life. In fact, neither of them is actually guaranteed for every person. Some people avoid paying taxes and others will be raptured, eluding the grim reaper. But according to Jesus Christ, what is certain is that every word of God will be fulfilled, down to the tiniest letter stroke (Matthew 5:18; 24:35; Luke 16:17; Revelation 1:4-5,19;

22:6). You can count on this, my friend—Jesus Christ *is* coming again, just as He said He would.

Third, what we understand about God, His eternal purpose, and our salvation is presently limited (1 John 3:2). Our finite minds cannot possibly comprehend the full measure of what is to be revealed to us one day. As Paul wrote, "For now we see in a mirror dimly, but then face to face; now I know in part, but then I will know fully just as I also have been fully known" (1 Corinthians 13:12). Our knowledge and experience are presently partial, but one day they will be made complete and full. This is God's way of saying, "Hang on. You ain't seen nothing yet!"

Finally, fixing our hope on Jesus and His return has a purifying effect on all of us (1 John 3:3). One way a bride prepares for her wedding day is by purifying herself. She does this by walking away from all other loves and dependent relationships. Though she may have been previously pursued or courted by many men, only one man now occupies her mind and attention. She is now and henceforth spoken for and set apart. In anticipation of her wedding, she keeps herself sexually pure, protecting her innocence. And all that she is she commits to her future husband.

Because we are Christ's bride, we also must purify ourselves as we anticipate His return. The word John uses for "purifies" in 1 John 3:3 is from *hagnizōō*, an uncommon word in the New Testament. It is used only one other time, and by the same author. John 11:55 speaks of Jews in Jesus's day *purifying* themselves in preparation for the Passover. In the Septuagint (Greek translation of the Old Testament), the word is used twice, once referring to newly freed Hebrews preparing themselves to encounter God at Mt. Sinai, and the other to the Levites purifying themselves from sin before presenting the tabernacle offerings.

Without question, there is a cause-effect relationship between hoping in Jesus's appearance and the purity of our lives. But what does this purity look like? Fortunately, John gives us a huge clue in verse 3. There he says our purity should mirror that of Jesus. And what do we know about the purity of Jesus?

We know that, as the God-Man, His was a life free from sin (1 Peter 2:22). And though we will not live sinless lives, our sensitivity to sin and our ability to resist and overcome it should increase with our spiritual maturity. Peter exhorts us, "As obedient children, do not be conformed to the former lusts which were yours in your ignorance, but like the Holy One who called you, be holy yourselves also in all your behavior; because it is written, 'You shall be holy, for I am holy'" (1 Peter 1:14-16).

Again, we are God's children, and children naturally inherit their parents' traits via DNA. Peter echoes this truth, adding that we are "partakers of the divine nature, having escaped the corruption that is in the world by lust" (2 Peter 1:4).

Following John's admonition for purity in light of the Lord's coming, he writes, "No one who is born of God practices sin, because His seed abides in him; and he cannot sin, because he is born of God. By this the children of God and the children of the devil are obvious: anyone who does not practice righteousness is not of God, nor the one who does not love his brother" (1 John 3:9-10).

So there is definitely an aspect of personal holiness associated with this concept of purity.

Second, Jesus was also fully dependent upon the Father for everything. Though He was 100 percent God, Christ chose as a Man to submit Himself to God. This is how He lived His earthly life—hearing from the Father and then telling it to others (John 3:11; 12:49). Christ spent long periods of time in communion with God the Father, and on more than one occasion, withdrew by Himself to pray (Luke 5:16; 6:12; 22:41-44; Hebrews 5:7). Humanly speaking, His constant communication with the Father was part of what guarded and nurtured His dependence on the One who had sent Him.

Finally, Jesus's agenda was also not His own, but this, too, came from the Father. In John 6:38, Jesus tells His disciples, "For I have come down from heaven, not to do My own will, but the will of Him who sent Me" (cf. Luke 22:42). The Son of God came to earth to fulfill a mission given to Him by the Father: "For God did not send the Son into the world to judge the world, but that the world might be saved through Him" (John 3:17; cf. 3:31-36).

An aspect of our purity involves knowing and seeking God's plan for our lives. Pursuing His plan keeps us from chasing our own. And we can be sure that His will for us is always "good and acceptable and perfect" (Romans 12:2). What drove Jesus's decisions were those things His Father desired. His delight was in Him, and in return He gave Jesus the desires that brought the most glory to God (Psalm 37:4; John 17:4). The Messiah had a singular ambition, something even more important to Him than eating. His constant passion was to "do the will of Him who sent Me and to accomplish His work" (John 4:34; cf. 5:30; 8:29; 17:4). Put simply—what pleased Him was to please His Father.

Can you say the same?

This purifying focus of Jesus's heart, life, and ministry unmistakably marked Him. This singular desire to bring glory to the Father consumed Him, so much so that at the end of His life He could look back with no regrets, knowing that He had glorified God on the earth and accomplished the work He had given Him to do (John 17:4). Christ's earthly life is our model and His future return is our motivation (1 John 2:6; Luke 6:40,46). And He wants His bride to be pure and prepared for Him. Knowing Him through His Word is preparation. A life free from sin's bondage is preparation. Daily dependence upon the Father is preparation. And following the Lord's agenda for our lives keeps us on track and focused on the things that really matter.

From what we understand from Scripture and see happening in the world around us, we appear to be living in the last days. This realization does not induce anxiety or produce panic. And it certainly does not foster complacency. To the contrary, it emboldens our faith, inspiring us with a sense of purposeful urgency. More than any previous Christian generation, I believe ours is seeing the legitimate foreshadowing of Revelation's realities. While we cannot be certain about the timing and fulfillment of these prophecies, we can be sure that the conditions are right for Revelation's arrival.

Because of these realities, Bible prophecy is more relevant to the church today than at any time since it was originally recorded thousands of years ago. Therefore, we cannot ignore it, shove it out of the way, or relegate it to an obscure theological church closet. Instead, we must engage these life-changing truths, obey them, and encourage one another with them. And we must allow them to motivate us toward a different kind of lifestyle.

Turn the Key and Enter

You have now been given ten keys to unlock the secrets of Bible prophecy. Every chapter of this book has placed a strategic key in your hand. Now you must do something with them. Keys are meant to unlock doors, but it doesn't end there. They are a means to a greater end. They open those doors so you can pass through to another place. These keys enable you to begin a journey of exploration into God's prophetic truth. But they also provide you a path through which you can experience some of the unique benefits that come when you continue using them in your daily life.

When Paul wrote to the Thessalonians, they were a church rocked by anxiety and confusion. And much of it was due to misinformation and false teaching about future Bible prophecy. Among his last words to them in that first letter, he writes, "Do not quench the Spirit; do not despise prophetic utterances. But examine everything carefully; hold fast to that which is good; abstain from every form of evil" (1 Thessalonians 5:19-22).

The "prophetic utterances" Paul mentions here can signify both spoken and written divine revelation (See Matthew 13:14; Acts 11:27-28; 1 Timothy 1:18-19; 4:14; 2 Peter 1:19-21; Revelation 1:3; 22:7,10,18-19). In the Thessalonian church, false teachers were abusing God's truth, just as they do today. Working in concert with their father the devil, they create counterfeit realities, and this sows confusion within the body of Christ. In our culture (and even within the church), the prophetic utterances found in God's Word are often despised because of unbiblical speculation and the abuse of charlatans. These counterfeit teachers and their "truths" are used as justification for those who declare the Bible and its prophecies to be invalid. But keep in mind, the existence of counterfeit currency presupposes there is an authentic original. There can't be a forgery without an original.

Therefore, as Paul exhorted us, we must "examine everything carefully," using the Bible itself as our standard. He tells the Thessalonians, and us, that when God's prophetic truth is ignored, dismissed, or disregarded, the Spirit is quenched. That's the equivalent of dousing the flame of a roaring fire. Instead, we must feed the Holy Spirit's fire in our lives and churches, not put it out. Our attitude should always be, "Let the Word speak!"

When the ink from John's quill dried after he wrote the last verse of his apocalyptic vision, the canon of Scripture officially came to a close. Because of this, we no longer have need for new "words from God." What we have, bound between Genesis and Revelation, is more than sufficient to give us what we need concerning "the knowledge of His will," and everything we need "pertaining to life and godliness" (Ephesians 4:11-16; Colossians 1:9-12; 2 Peter 1:1-3). May we hold with high regard every word of God contained in that Holy Scripture. And that certainly includes those prophetic utterances that have yet to see their fulfillment.

Far beyond merely gathering fascinating facts about the end of days, prophecy reminds us we are headed for both a destination *and* a destiny. The destination is heaven, but our destiny is Jesus Himself. Ultimately, Bible prophecy prepares us to meet Christ and be with Him forever. And that's no secret. Therefore, I encourage you to live the kind of life that prepares you for your future glorious encounter with Him. Allow Bible prophecy to inspire you toward intimacy with

Jesus, the very One on whom your hope is fixed. I encourage you to carry these keys with you, using them to help yourself and other believers as we all prepare to see Jesus "just as He is"!

Maranatha!

Endnotes

Introduction: Why Study Bible Prophecy?

1. The Greek word for "disciple" (*mathetes*) primarily means "learner."

2. Cheryl K. Chumley, "4 in 10 American adults: We're living in the end times," *Washington Times*, September 12, 2013, www.washingtontimes.com/news/2013/sep/12/4-in10-american-adults-were-living-end-times/.

Chapter 1: Understanding the Nature of Prophecy

1. "Top Ten Reasons Why Pastors Don't Preach on Bible Prophecy," from Jeff Kinley, *The End of America? Bible Prophecy and a Country in Crisis* (Eugene, OR: Harvest House, 2017), 34-35.

   1. The pastor doesn't feel qualified to teach on the subject.

   2. Preaching on prophecy requires hard work and much study. Some pastors may get by more on personality than having diligently studied the Word. Some pastors busy themselves with meetings, leadership duties, and church activities, leaving little room to do what God has actually called them to.

   3. Prophecy is sometimes viewed as controversial, sensational, and for some, even frightening and offensive. There are enough obstacles pastors face with their congregations without creating more distance between the pulpit and the pew.

   4. There are divergent views on eschatology within the body of Christ. As such, it is often seen as divisive, and therefore avoided.

   5. To be too dogmatic or confident regarding prophetic interpretation can come off as prideful, or even cult-like at times.

   6. The end times involves God's wrath, and some pastors don't want to be viewed as a prophet of doom. Negativity tends to *empty* seats, not fill them.

   7. No one *really* knows the future, so why dwell on it?

   8. Many pastors and denominations do not believe in a literal, prophetic fulfillment of Scripture. Rather, they take a spiritual or symbolic approach when interpreting books like Revelation or Daniel.

   9. There are so many more *relevant* things to preach on (marriage, handling stress, family issues, personal problems, etc.).

   10. Perhaps for some, they fear people will stop giving financially if they think the world is ending soon.

2. See also Romans 5:9; 8:1; Revelation 3:10; 1 Thessalonians 4:15-18. As those who trust in Jesus for salvation, we are spared from all forms of God's wrath, whether it be eschatological or eternal.

Chapter 2: Don't Misread the Signs

1. Paul's point here was that having knowledge, devoid of love for our brother or sister, only makes us feel good about ourselves, thus making us arrogant. Knowledge and love work together to build up the body of Christ.

Chapter 3: Developing Biblical Discernment

1. See at www.evlio.com/the-amount-of-information-on-the-internet-is-staggering/.

2. See at http://blog.qmee.com/qmee-online-in-60-seconds/.

3. Stephanie Pappas, "How Big Is the Internet, Really?" *LiveScience*, March 18, 2016, www
.livescience.com/54094-how-big-is-the-internet.html.

4. See also Romans 2:1-6.

5. John MacArthur, "Principles for Discernment, Part 1," *Grace to You*, November 8, 2002,
www.gty.org/library/sermons-library/TMC209/principles-for-discernment-part-1.

6. "State of the Bible 2017: Top Findings," *Barna*, April 4, 2017, www.barna.com/research/
state-bible-2017-top-findings/.

7. "Top 10 Findings on Teens and the Bible," *Barna*, August 26, 2016, www.barna.com/
research/top-10-findings-teens-bible/#.V8Gwga0om_4.

8. Lydia Saad, "Sermon Content Is What Appeals Most to Churchgoers," *Gallup*, April 14,
2017, http://news.gallup.com/poll/208529/sermon-content-appeals-churchgoers.aspx.

9. In our natural, sinful condition, none of us seeks after God (Romans 3:10-12). Those who
do come to Christ do so because the Father has drawn them to Him (John 6:37,44,65).
Therefore, it follows that those who utilize the common discernment given to them by
God are among those whom the Father has chosen for salvation (Ephesians 1:4-6).

10. Some moral or religious-minded non-Christians may subscribe to God's basic moral law.
This is a result of not rejecting God's creative and conscience-based revelation of Himself.
However, once past these fundamental truths, an understanding and embracing of the
rest of God's revelation (as found in Scripture) eludes them as far as engaging with their
spirit (which is dead).

11. The APGAR score stands for: Appearance (skin color), Pulse (heart rate), Grimace
response (reflexes), Activity (muscle tone), and Respiration (breathing rate and effort).

12. John MacArthur, *Hebrews* (Chicago: Moody Press, 1983), 134.

13. Walter Bauer, William Arndt, F. Wilbur Gingrich, *A Greek-English Lexicon of the New Testament and Other Early Christian Literature* (Chicago: University of Chicago Press, 1979),
56, 185.

14. Bauer et al, *Greek-English Lexicon of the New Testament*, 400.

15. The original Greek verb is (*gumnazō*), and literally means to "train or practice naked" in
ancient Greek athletic competition.

16. The word is also used in Hebrews 12:11 referring to God's discipline (training) of His
children.

Chapter 4: Spotting Counterfeit Truth

1. Compare Deuteronomy 18:20-22 with Jeremiah 28:9 and Ezekiel 33:33.

2. Among those false prophets listed in the Old Testament are: Balaam (Numbers 22–24),
Zedekiah (1 Kings 22:11-28), Hananiah (Jeremiah 28:1-17), Shemaiah (Jeremiah 29:24-
32), Ahab and Zedekiah (Jeremiah 29:21-23), Noadiah (Nehemiah 6:14), and others
(Ezekiel 13).

3. Paul spent about three years establishing the church at Ephesus on his third missionary
journey (Acts 19). He had earlier left Priscilla and Aquila there while on his second missionary journey (Acts 18:18-19).

4. Paul wrote this letter from Corinth, where false teachers were also in plentiful supply.

5. This issue was at the center of the controversy at the church in Jerusalem early on in Acts 15.

6. This is why the apostle feared the Corinthians would be led astray from the simplicity and purity of devotion to Christ (2 Corinthians 11:3). This would occur, he says, through a Satanic-like deception of preaching "another Jesus," and the promotion of a different gospel from the one Paul had presented to them (11:4).

7. Paul uses the Greek word *anathema*, referring to eternal damnation. See Romans 9:3; 1 Corinthians 12:3; 16:22.

8. He even suggests that if these Judaizers loved circumcision so much as proof and part of their salvation, then they should demonstrate their total commitment to God by completely castrating themselves! (Galatians 5:11-12).

9. "Dogs" was a term many Jews used to describe Gentiles, whom they disdained as filthy animals.

10. Just as Paul wrote to the Ephesian church through his letters to Timothy, he addressed issues in the church at Crete through his letter to Titus.

11. Homer Kent, *The Pastoral Epistles* (Chicago: Moody Press, 1982), 218.

12. See also 1 Timothy 4:1; James 5:3; 1 Peter 4:7; 2 Peter 3:3-4; Jude 17-18.

13. For more on this subject, see Mark Hitchcock and Jeff Kinley, *The Coming Apostasy: Exposing the Sabotage of Christianity from Within* (Carol Stream, IL: Tyndale House, 2017).

14. Jude along with James were the half-brothers of Jesus (Matthew 13:55; Mark 6:3).

15. The participle used by Jude was sometimes used to describe apocalyptic visions experienced both by true and false prophets. NET Bible, footnote, p. 2263.

16. Compare 2 Peter 2:10. The idea may be that they flippantly address demons with a false bravado masquerading as spiritual authority. Commanding demons and "binding Satan" is popular among some prosperity gospel preachers today.

17. Compare Genesis 4:1-8.

18. Compare Numbers 22–25; 2 Peter 2:15.

19. Compare Numbers 16:1-35.

20. Some translate "hidden reefs" as "stains" as in 2 Peter 2:13.

21. This prophesy, inspired by the Holy Spirit to Jude, is also recorded in the noncanonical book of Enoch.

22. The Nicolaitans are believed to be followers of Nicolas, a man from Antioch who is chosen as a deacon in the church at Jerusalem in Acts 6. Clement of Alexandria wrote that these immoral church members "abandoned themselves to pleasure like goats, leading a life of self-indulgence." Philip Schaff, *The Sacred Writings of Clement of Alexandria, Vol. 1* (Jazzybee Verlag, 2017).

23. Compare Jude 23 here.

Chapter 5: Cracking the Bible Code

1. Most likely in 1 Thessalonians, Paul is referring to the shofar used in ancient Israel to gather God's people together. This is precisely what will occur at the rapture, as the bride is summoned to gather together with the dead in Christ.

2. Mark Hitchcock, *The End* (Carol Stream, IL: Tyndale House, 2012), 55.

3. Some see Babylon itself as symbolic or representative, though Scripture never explains it as such. This leads many Bible scholars to interpret that Babylon is an actual city.

4. "Five have fallen" (Egypt, Babylon, Assyria, Medo-Persia, Greece), "one is" (Rome in John's day), and "the other has not yet come" (antichrist's ten-kingdom confederation in Revelation 17:12).

5. J. Dwight Pentecost, *Things to Come* (Grand Rapids, MI: Zondervan Publishing House, 1964), 46-47.

6. This prophecy is also known as the protoevangelium or the first mention of the gospel.

7. During the intertestamental period, this ruthless Greek king outlawed Jewish worship, and following a Jewish rebellion, invaded the Jewish temple, setting up a statue of Zeus and sacrificing a pig on the altar. He also slaughtered a large number of Jews. See 1 Maccabees 1–2.

Chapter 6: Exploring Scripture's Unfulfilled Prophecies

1. This word is used to describe both the rapture and the second coming in the New Testament. Scriptures where it refers to the rapture include: 1 Corinthians 15:23; 1 Thessalonians 2:19; 4:15; 5:23; James 5:7-8; 2 Peter 3:3-4,11-12; 1 John 2:28.

2. Of the 14 times this powerful word is used in the New Testament, five of those instances mean to "disappear" or to be "caught up to heaven." It's the same word used to describe Philip being snatched away and suddenly appearing in a different location, Paul being caught up into the third heaven, and Jesus's own ascension (Acts 8:39-40; 2 Corinthians 12:2-4; Revelation 12:5)

3. Among the many reasons for a later (AD 95) writing of Revelation are (1) this has been the dominant view of the church for 1,900 years, including many of the early church fathers; (2) it is believed the church at Smyrna (Revelation 2:8-11) did not even exist in AD 65; (3) in AD 65 the church at Laodicea (3:14-22) was still recovering from a massive earthquake that occurred in AD 60, so they wouldn't have thought themselves at that time as "rich...and have need of nothing" (3:17); and (4) had John been arrested by Nero (AD 54–68), he would have likely been killed (as were Peter and Paul) and not banished in exile as he was under Domitian's reign (AD 81–96).

4. Contrary to common belief, the rapture does not signify the beginning of the seven-year tribulation. Antichrist's peace treaty does. Scripture marks the midpoint of these seven years with the abomination of desolation, which occurs three-and-a-half years from this peace agreement, not from the moment of the rapture (Daniel 7:25; 9:27; 12:7,11-13; Matthew 24:15-21). Though the rapture won't officially begin the tribulation, it will help to trigger chaotic global events and the need for a world leader to emerge and bring peace and safety to the world.

5. Mark Hitchcock, *The End* (Carol Stream, IL: Tyndale House, 2012), 309.

6. See at www.idfblog.com/facts-figures/rocket-attacks-toward-israel/.

7. Some attempt to apply Esther 9 as a fulfillment of this prophecy. However, the parallels are superficial and quickly break down.

8. Jehoshaphat means "Yahweh has judged."

9. The gospel will be preached during the tribulation period by the two witnesses (Revelation

11:1-14), the 144,000 male Jewish evangelists (Revelation 14:1-5), and the angel who flies over the earth urging repentance (Revelation 14:6-7).

10. Tribulation Jews who were unwise stewards of the salvation truth given them are cast into outer darkness, where there is "weeping and gnashing of teeth" (Matthew 25:30).

11. When the "legion" of demons was confronted by Christ in the country of the Gerasenes, they begged Jesus not to send them into the "abyss" (Luke 8:30-31).

12. In Luke 9:1 and Matthew 10:1, Jesus sent out the Twelve, giving them power over demons and disease. This was a supernatural enabling to further authenticate Christ and His kingdom message of salvation. However, this miracle-working power is not given to us today, for if it were, we could eradicate disease and demonic influence in the world. Jesus told His disciples not to glory in their authority over demons, but instead to rejoice that their names were written in heaven (Luke 10:20).

13. This is not the same Gog and Magog of Ezekiel 38. Here the terms refer to more of an adjectival phrase representing those who oppose God and His people. Like saying "Armageddon Part II."

14. Here are six facts worth noting about this lake of fire:

    1. It's real, as real as heaven (Revelation 20:10,14-15; 21:8).

    2. It's everlasting (Matthew 18:8; 25:41).

    3. It's inescapable because God Himself imprisons you there (Revelation 14:9-11).

    4. It's unquenchable. You burn, but you don't burn up (Mark 9:43-48).

    5. It's unimaginable. The torment in "Lake Hell" is inconceivable to mortal minds because it involves the wrath of an infinite God. Jesus also warned that hell would be a place of "weeping and gnashing of teeth," describing the unrelenting pain (Matthew 8:12; 13:42; 22:13; 24:51; 25:30).

    6. It's *hot*. It is described as "fire" for a reason. But just how hot is this lake of fire? It is safe to say that it is immeasurably hot...*wrathfully* hot. And fueled, not by physical elements, but with supernatural flame and fury. For those who die without Christ, this "second death" is their eternal experience (Revelation 20:14).

    Some may object to a "cruel God" who would allow His creation to suffer so, even worse to send them to such a place. But remember that God is not like us. He is just and righteous, and His character and ways are far above ours (Isaiah 55:8-9). And His judgments are based upon our response to His person and holy law. Some may protest saying this is unfair. But which is more unfair: God throwing unrepentant sinners into a justly deserved eternal torment *or* that same God sending His beloved Son to suffer a "lake of fire" wrath on the cross so that we could know Him and never have to experience one ounce of His righteous fury (Romans 5:6-8; 2 Corinthians 5:21; 1 Peter 3:18)?

Chapter 7: Examining the Major Views on Prophecy

1. Martin Hughes, "Christians Hardly Read the Bible Themselves. Why Do They Try So Hard to Force It on Others?," *Patheos*, October 25, 2015, www.patheos.com/blogs/barrierbreaker/why-do-christians-who-rarely-read-the-bible-themselves-try-so-hard-to-push-it-on-to-others/.

2. "The State of the Bible: 6 Trends for 2014," *Barna*, April 8, 2014, www.barna.com/research/the-state-of-the-bible-6-trends-for-2014/.

3. Jesus is at the right hand of the throne of God in heaven. But He is not yet reigning upon the Davidic throne of the millennial kingdom.

4. Pentecost, *Things to Come,* 374.

5. John F. Walvoord, "Amillenniallism from Augustine to Modern Times," *Bible.org,* bible.org/seriespage/4-amillenniallism-augustine-modern-times.

6. In Revelation 5:11, John uses another number, "myriads," which is the number 10,000 in Greek. But rather than communicate a specific number, in its context here John is expressing a number that is beyond calculation and comprehension. That is why he multiplies it by itself. He is being somewhat vague by using the plural form of this number, intending to communicate that the number of the angels and the redeemed were *innumerable.* In fact, elsewhere, the same word is used to express this numerically vague concept in Luke 12:1 and Hebrews 12:22.

7. Jeff Kinley, *Wake the Bride* (Eugene, OR: Harvest House, 2015).

8. There is an increasing chronological intensity with the seal, trumpet, and bowl judgments of Revelation. However, the pretribulational view sees all of Revelation's wrath as coming from God. Therefore, a rescue which is "pre," or before, the tribulation.

9. Mark Hitchcock, *The End* (Carol Stream, IL: Tyndale House, 2012), 140.

10. "Timing of the Rapture," *PreWrath Ministries,* https://prewrathministries.org/timing-of-the-rapture/.

11. For more on this powerful analogy, see Jeff Kinley, *Wake the Bride* (Eugene, OR: Harvest House, 2015), 69-72.

12. The reasons many scholars see the 24 elders as representative of the church are as follows: Like the description Scripture gives of the church, the 24 elders have been given crowns (Revelation 2:10; 3:11; 4:4,10; 1 Corinthians 9:25; 1 Thessalonians 2:19; 2 Timothy 4:8; James 1:12; 1 Peter 5:4). They are clothed in white garments (Revelation 4:4; 19:7-8). Tribulation saints are not yet saved, so it cannot refer to them. The only portion of God's family in heaven that meets this description is the raptured and resurrected church (Revelation 5:8-10).

Chapter 8: Investigating "Prophecy Apologetics"

1. See at www.internetworldstats.com/stats.htm.

2. In His parable of the rich man and Lazarus, when the tormented man requested to return from the grave in order to warn his brothers about that awful place, Abraham denies his request, citing, "They have Moses and the Prophets; let them hear them." But he said, "No, father Abraham, but if someone goes to them from the dead, they will repent!" But he said to him, "If they do not listen to Moses and the Prophets, they will not be persuaded even if someone rises from the dead."

3. "Americans Are Most Likely to Base Truth on Feelings," *Barna,* February 12, 2002, www.barna.com/research/americans-are-most-likely-to-base-truth-on-feelings/.

4. "'Nones' on the Rise," *Pew Research Center,* October 9, 2012, www.pewforum.org/2012/10/09/nones-on-the-rise/.

5. Lillian Kwon, "Survey: Churches Losing Youths Long Before College," *Christian Post,* June 29, 2009, www.christianpost.com/news/survey-churches-losing-youths-long-before-college-39433/.

6. Josh McDowell, *Evidence That Demands a Verdict, Part 1* (San Bernardino, CA: Campus Crusade for Christ, 1972), 84-88.

7. Alfred Edersheim, *Prophecy and History in Relation to the Messiah* (New York: Anson D. F. Randolph and Company, 1885).

8. Peter Stoner, *Science Speaks* (Chicago: Moody Press, 1969), 106-7.

9. Ibid., 109.

10. Ibid., 112.

11. "Vital Statistics: Jewish Population of the World," *Jewish Virtual Library*, www.jewish virtuallibrary.org/jsource/Judaism/jewpop.html.

12. "Here Are the Top Cashless Countries in the World," *Business Today*, December 29, 2016, www.businesstoday.in/current/economy-politics/here-are-the-top-cashless-countries-in -the-world/story/241430.html.

13. "The Christ Quake," *Evidence for God from Science*, November 10, 2013, http://discussions .godandscience.org/viewtopic.php?t=38866.

14. For an extensive study of the days of Noah and their relevance to modern times, see Jeff Kinley, *As It Was in the Days of Noah* (Eugene, OR: Harvest House, 2014).

Chapter 9: Building Up the Body of Christ

1. Bauer, Arndt, Gingrich, *A Greek-English Lexicon of the New Testament and Other Early Christian Literature* (Chicago: University of Chicago Press, 1979), 617.

2. Various contextual meanings of *parakaleo* in the New Testament include: to be called to one's side (Acts 28:20; Matthew 26:53; 2 Corinthians 12:8); to appeal to, urge, exhort (Acts 16:40; 2 Corinthians 5:20; 10:1; 1 Thessalonians 2:11; 5:11; Hebrews 3:13; Ephesians 4:1; Philippians 4:2; Titus 2:6; 1 Peter 2:11); to request, implore, appeal to (Matthew 8:5; 18:32; Mark 1:40; 2 Corinthians 12:18); to comfort, encourage, cheer up (2 Corinthians 1:4; 7:6; 1 Thessalonians 3:2; 4:18).

Chapter 10: Preparing for Jesus's Return

1. Mike Lockley, "200-Year-Old Mystery of Shugborough Code 'Solved,'" *Birmingham Post*, December 21, 2014, www.birminghampost.co.uk/news/ regional-affairs/200-year-old-mystery-shugborough-code-solved-8319385.

The End of America?

What happens when a country turns away from faith in God? Jeff Kinley explores historical and biblical precedents for the demise of a nation and offers valuable perspective on the future of America.

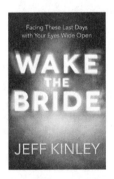

Wake the Bride

Many people are unaware of the signs of the times. Many others seem consumed by end-times hype. This innovative guide to the book of Revelation shows that our primary concern should not be the timing of Christ's return, but rather, the spirit and character He desires in His bride.

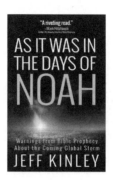

As It Was in the Days of Noah

This powerful book explores the similarities between Noah's day and ours, such as the rapid rise in evil and increasingly flagrant disregard for God. A captivating read that affirms the urgency of living wisely and "redeeming the time" as we see the last days drawing nearer.

To learn more about Harvest House books and
to read sample chapters, visit our website:

www.harvesthousepublishers.com

HARVEST HOUSE PUBLISHERS
EUGENE, OREGON